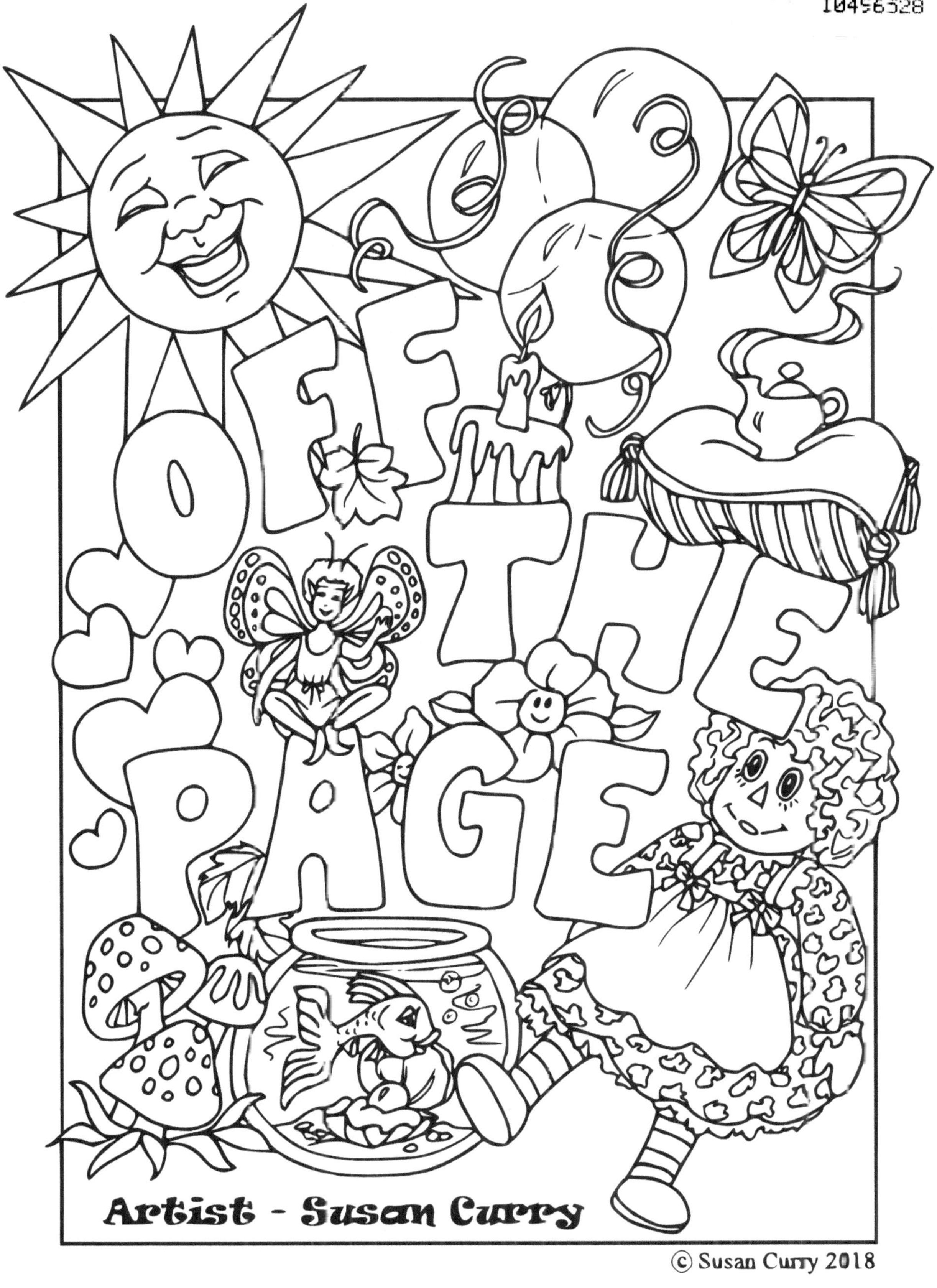

Also by Susan Curry

Living On Memory Lane
Visit with Nana and Papa on their lovely country farm.
- I love this coloring book! Living on Memory Lane is just that.....it's like reliving my childhood! I can relate to every picture Susan has drawn. And I am anxiously awaiting her next book! ~ Lisa D.., Dec. 13, 2016

The Adventures of Little Sister
Join in the wonderful memories of being an active Little Girl
- Being a little sister myself, I couldn't resist the subject matter of this book. You will also like that each page has it's own story about how it came to be. You wont be sorry.
~ Robin, Apr. 11, 2017

Adventures with the Country Cousins
Join Bud and Sis for a summer of growing up, on a visit to the family farm.
- I could easily give this book TEN stars with a big smile on my face as I did !!! Susan is a fabulous artist & a great storyteller! I found a little bit of my own life in this book. ~ Caleb's Granny, May 20, 2017

Christmas on Memory Lane
Wonderful memories of Christmas Past on Memory Lane
- The best Christmas book I have come across. Love all the drawings. Susan is such a talented artist! I have all her books to this collection, can't wait for her next book. Highly recommended! ~ Grandma E, October 11, 2017

* * * * *

OFF THE PAGE

Copyright © 2018 Susan Curry
All rights reserved.

In accordance with the U.S. Copyright Act of 1976, the scanning*, uploading, and electronic sharing of any part of this book without the permission of the artist/author constitutes unlawful piracy and theft of the artist/author's intellectual property. If you would like to use material from the book (other than for review purposes), prior written permission must be obtained by contacting the artist/author at:
*an exception is granted for PERSONAL USE ONLY scans and then only so long as any scanned or printed pages are NOT distributed in any manner to any other person, party or parties.

hanfordrose@yahoo.com

Or visit me on Facebook at: www.facebook.com/SueCurryArt

Thank You for your support of the artist/author's rights.

First Edition

ISBN: 9781726606684
ISBN-10: 1726606686

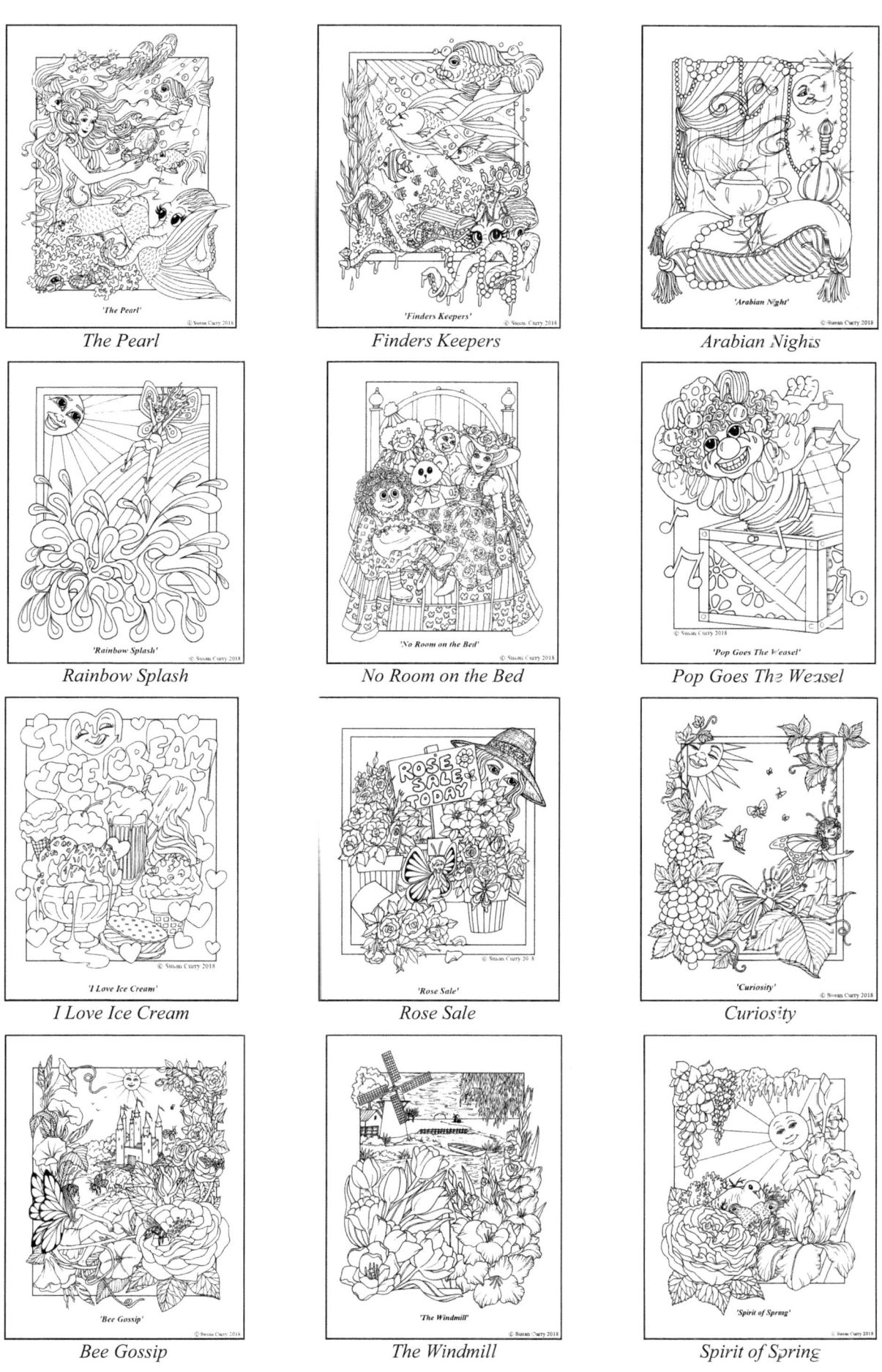

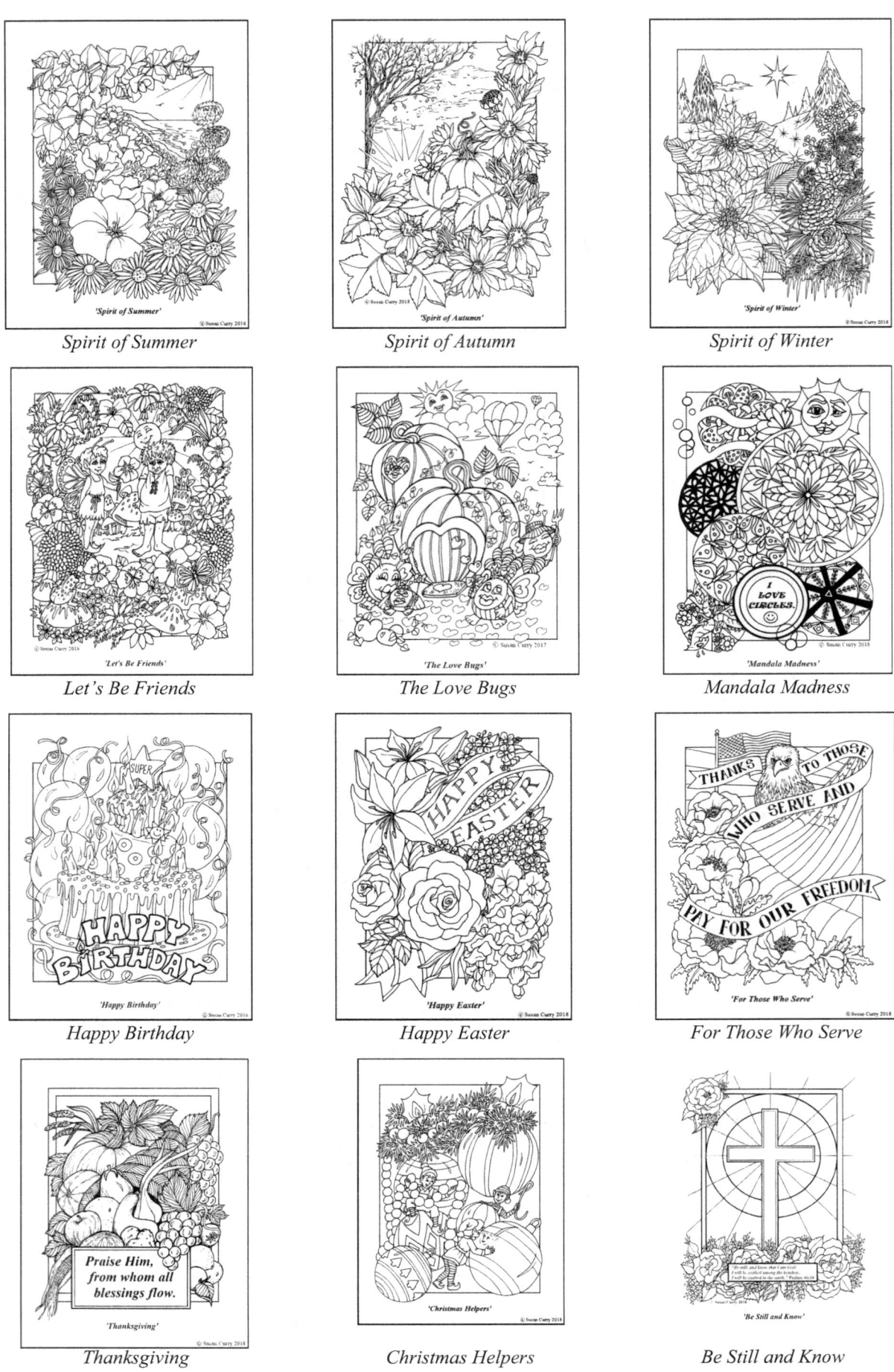

Spirit of Summer	*Spirit of Autumn*	*Spirit of Winter*
Let's Be Friends	*The Love Bugs*	*Mandala Madness*
Happy Birthday	*Happy Easter*	*For Those Who Serve*
Thanksgiving	*Christmas Helpers*	*Be Still and Know*

BONUS PAGES

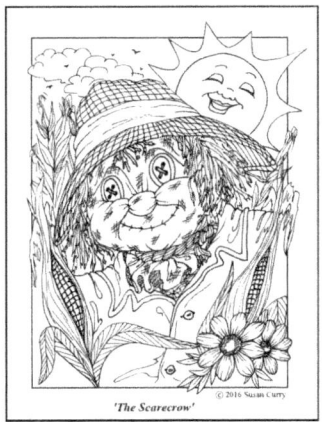

The Scarecrow
"Living on Memory Lane"

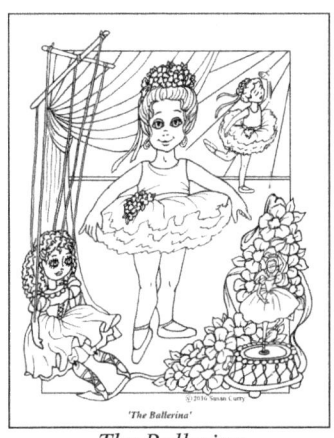

The Ballerina
"The Adventures of Little Sister"

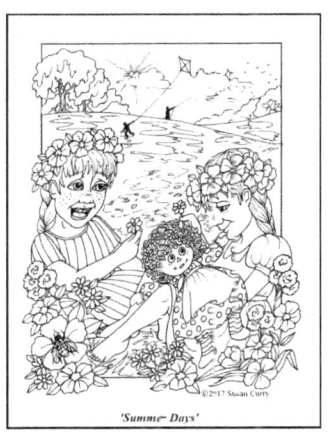

Summer Days
"Adventures with the Country Cousins"

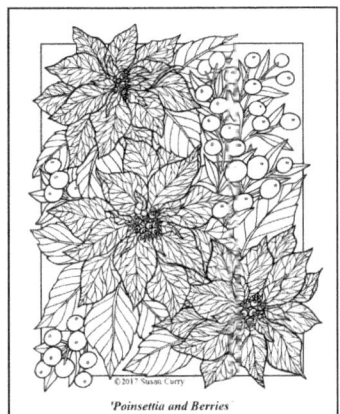

Poinsettia and Berries
"Christmas on Memory Lane"

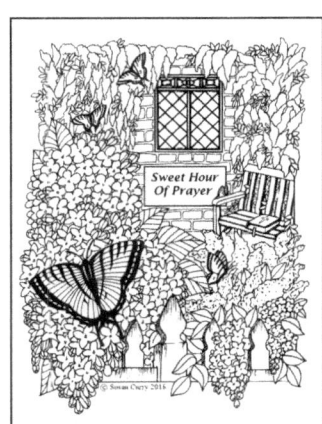

Sweet Hour of Prayer
"Sing, Color and Praise the Lord"
(Coming soon)

Dedicated to colorists everywhere!

IMPORTANT INFORMATION FOR USING THIS BOOK

- This book contains over 30 beautifully hand-drawn illustrations, SINGLE SIDED (back is blank), to color, accompanied by a 26 chapter Storybook.

- Beside a colorable Title Page and 'This Book Belongs To': Page, there are 26 full size illustrations to accompany each of the chapters in the Storybook, as well as BONUS PAGES from the Artist/Authors two previous works, PLUS a Preview drawing for the next book in the series 'Return to Memory Lane'.

- The pages are printed on #60 lb bright white paper which performs well for all brands of colored pencils and crayons, without the need of a blotter page.

- To avoid any "Uh Oh's" and the associated disappointment, **Marker and Gel Pen users are STRONGLY ENCOURAGED to USE A BLOTTER SHEET** behind the drawing to avoid any possibility of bleed through to the next page.

- Most IMPORTANT of all: Relax, have fun, stand-up and stretch often, and remember that sometimes the most beautiful things come from what we think at first are mistakes, but which turn out to be art's way of working magic!

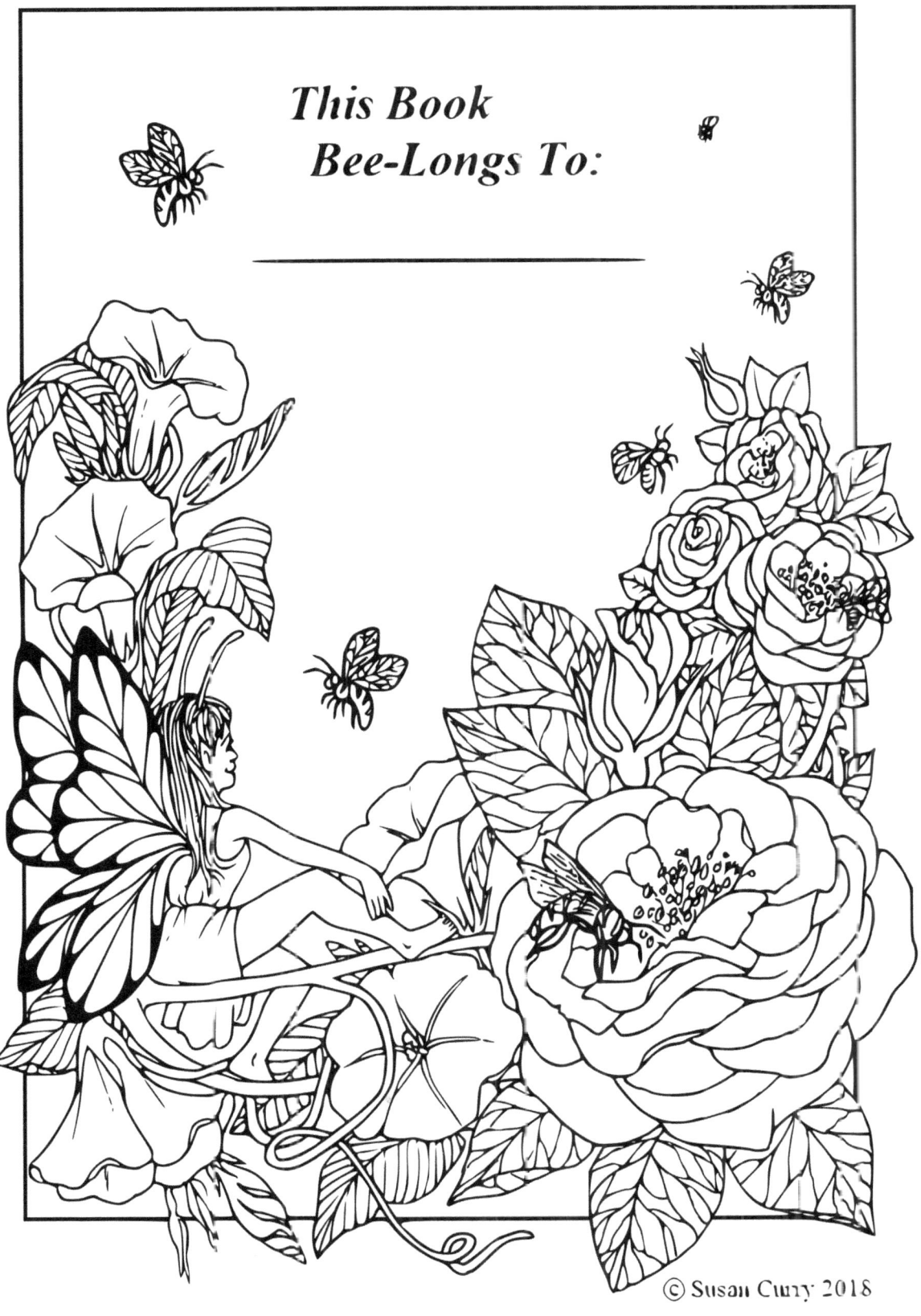

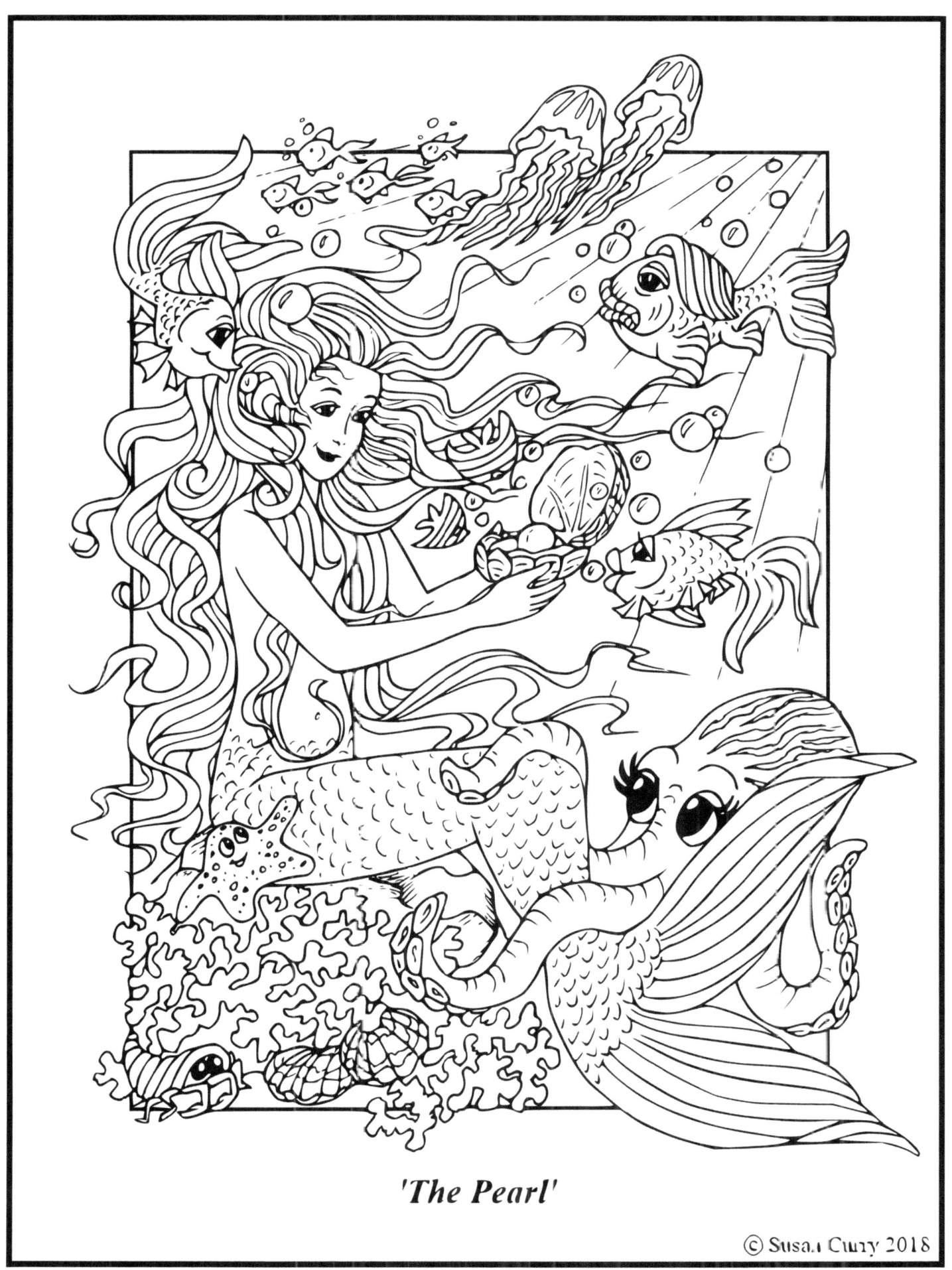

'The Pearl'

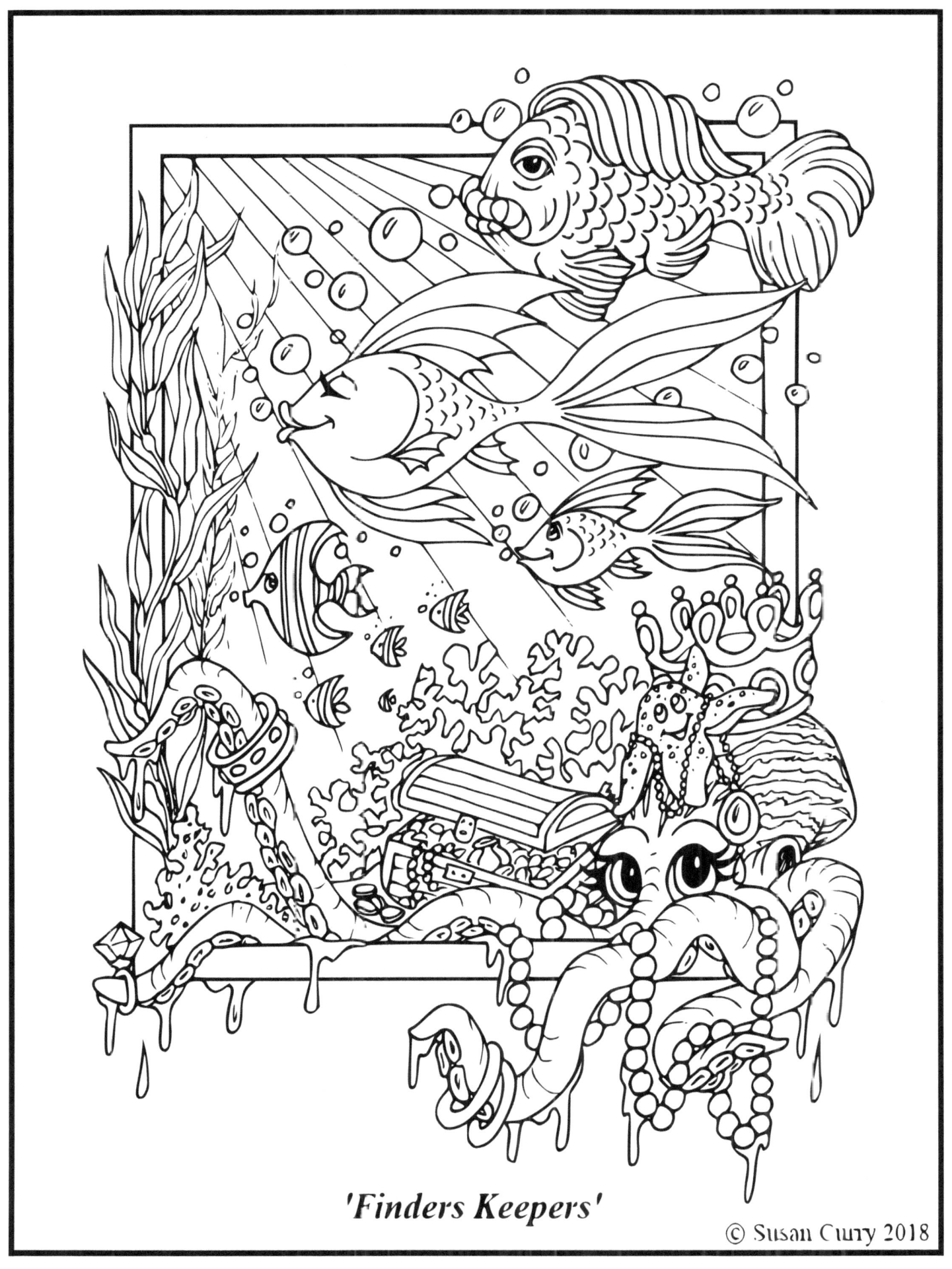

'Finders Keepers'

© Susan Curry 2018

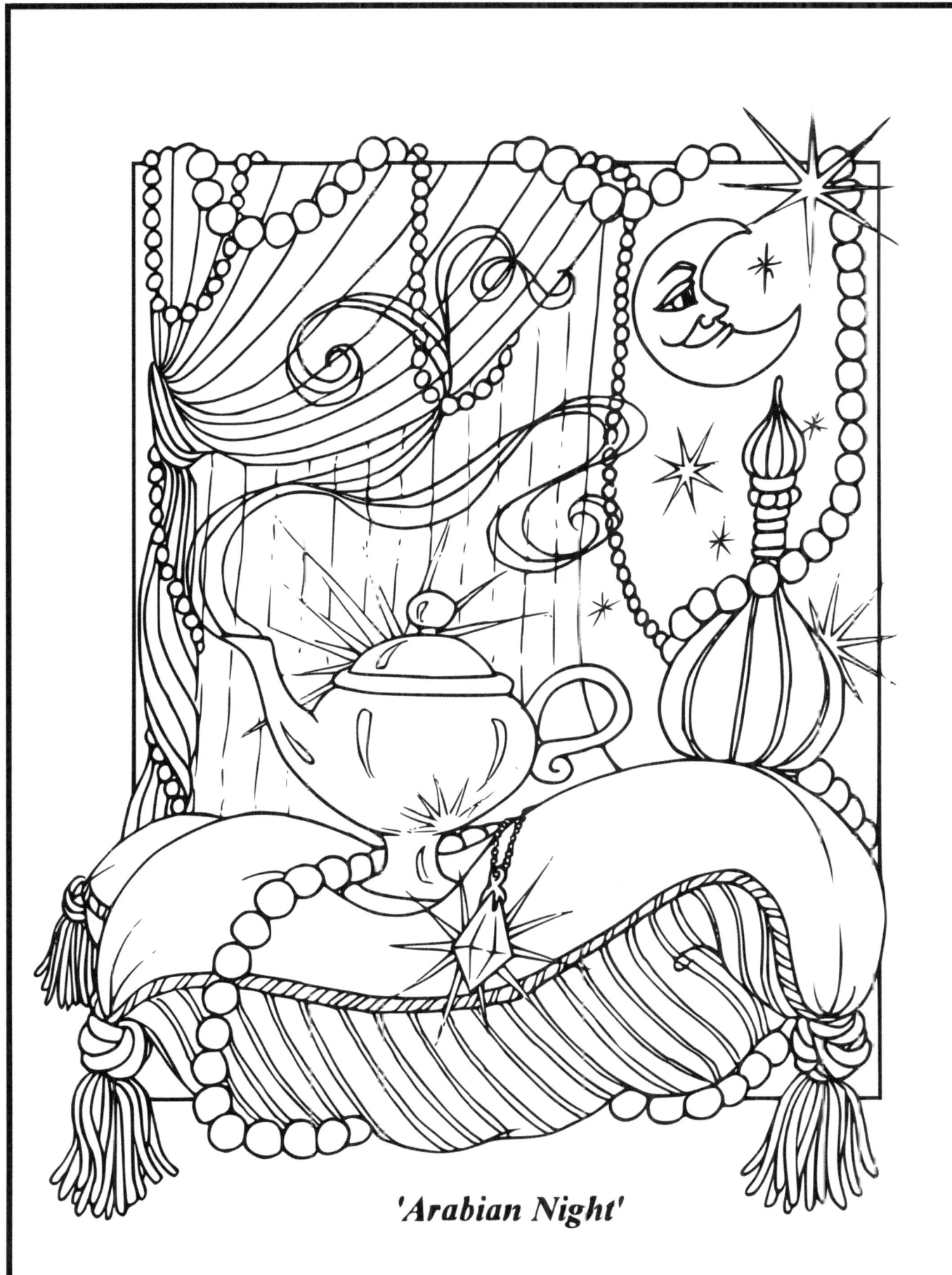
'Arabian Night'

© Susan Curry 2018

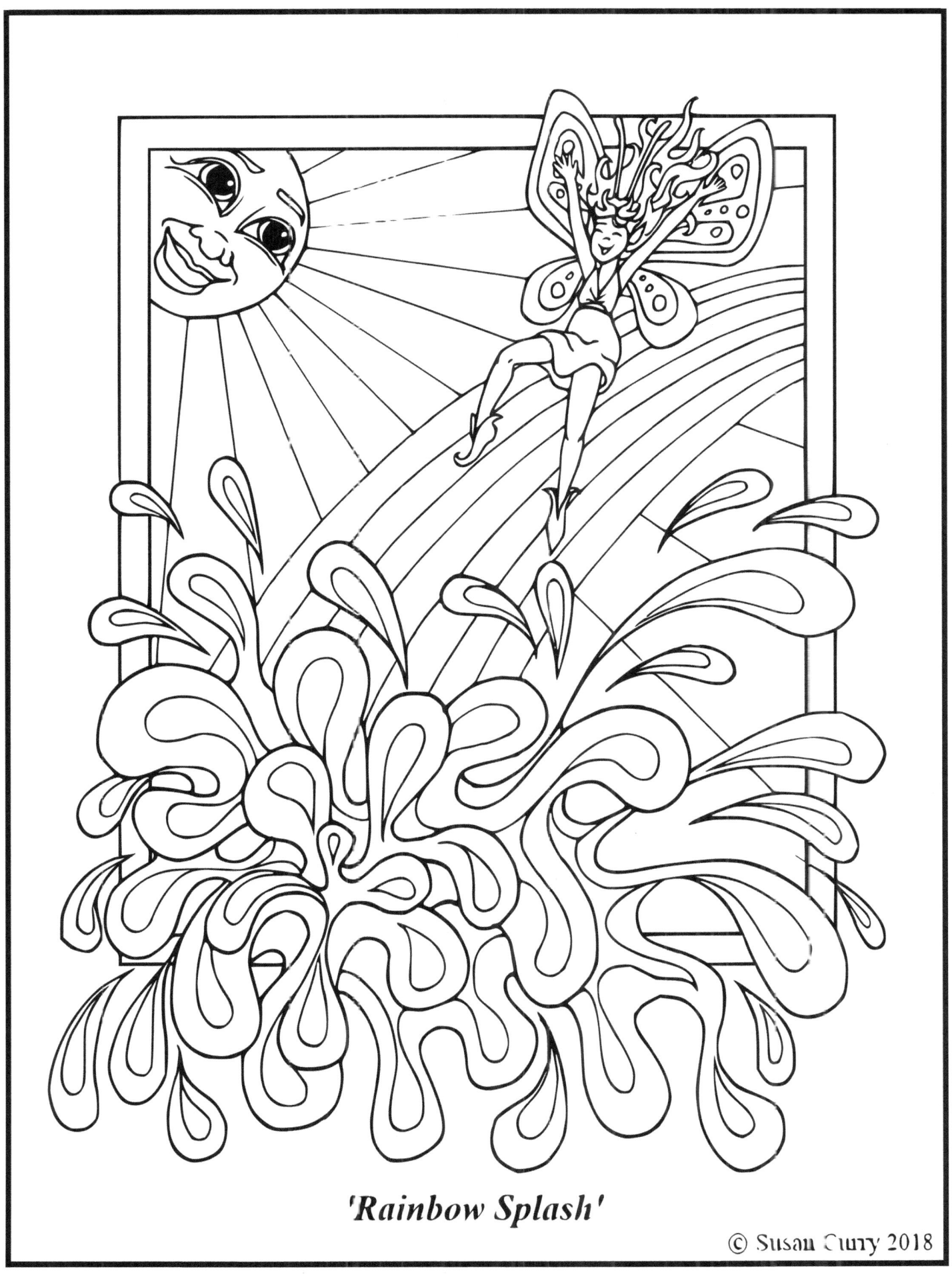

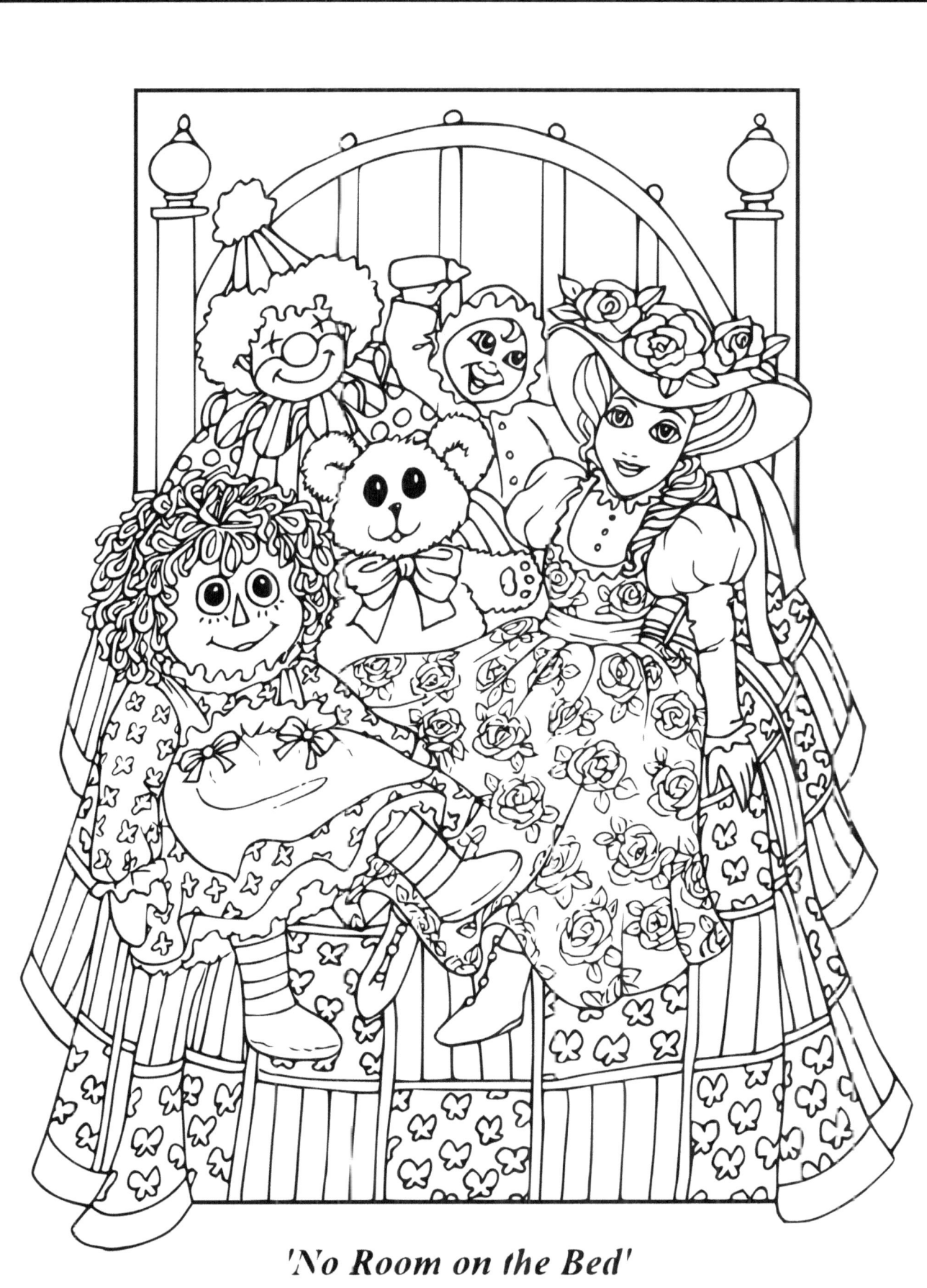

'No Room on the Bed'

© Susan Curry 2018

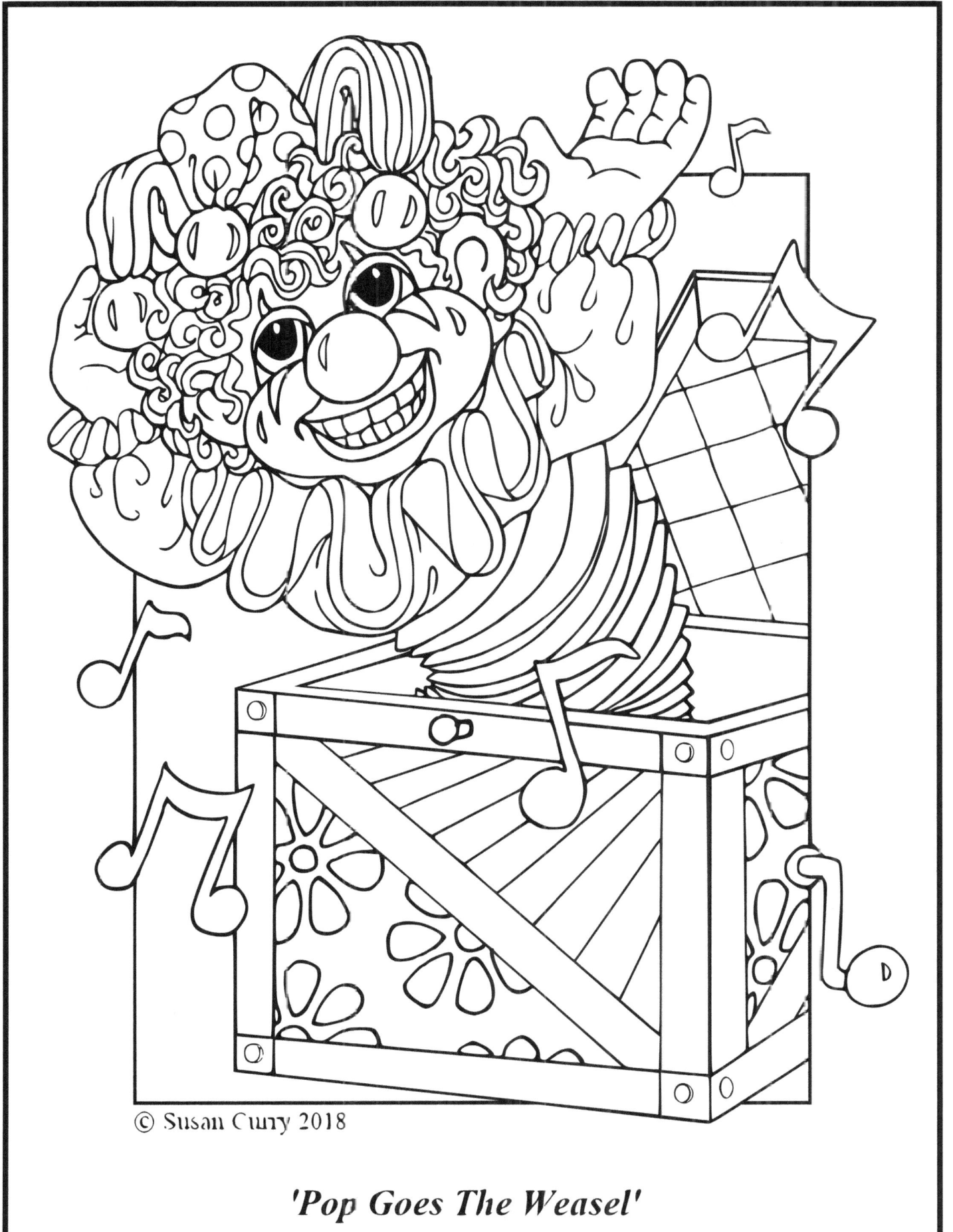

'Pop Goes The Weasel'

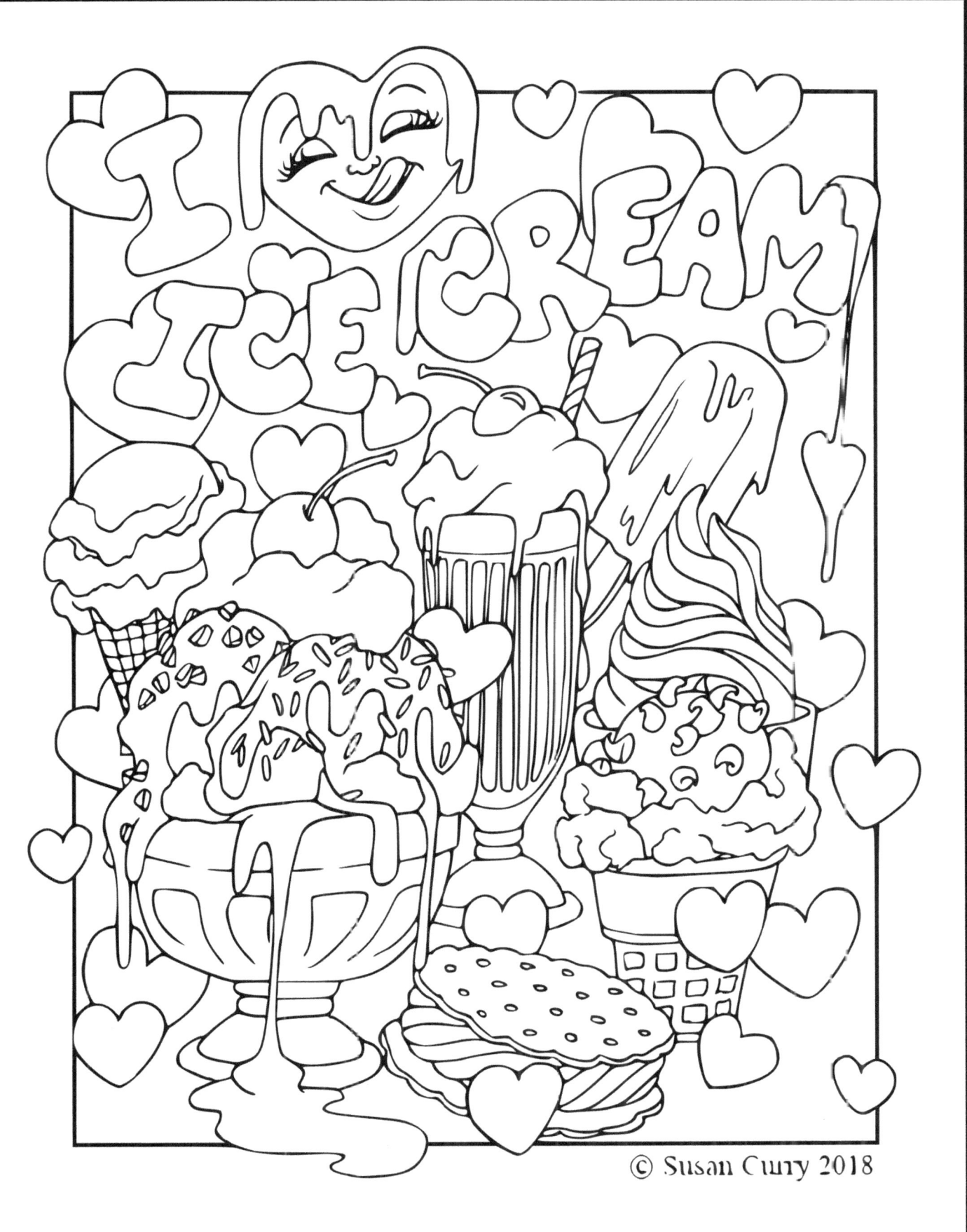

'I Love Ice Cream'

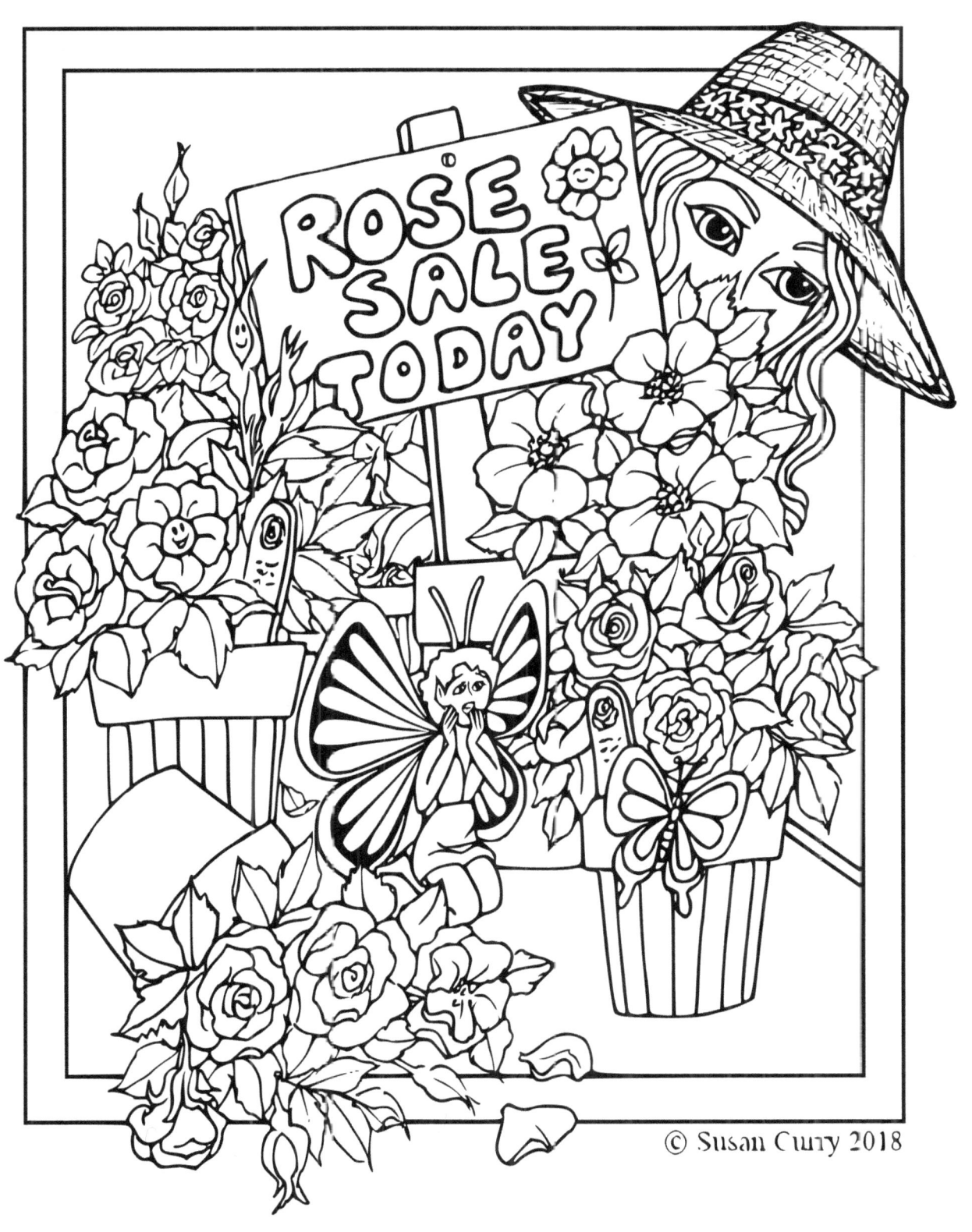

'Rose Sale'

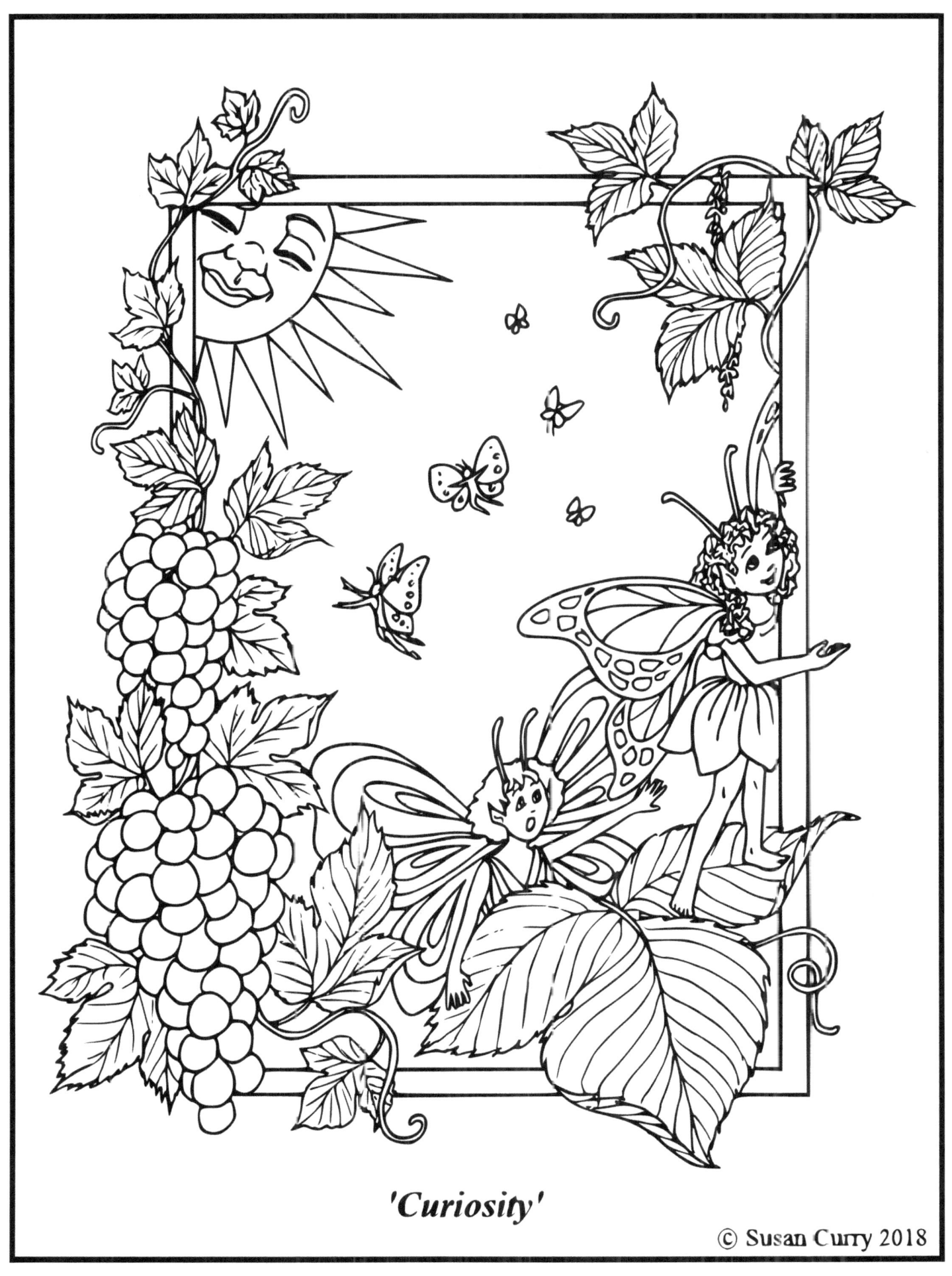

'Curiosity'

© Susan Curry 2018

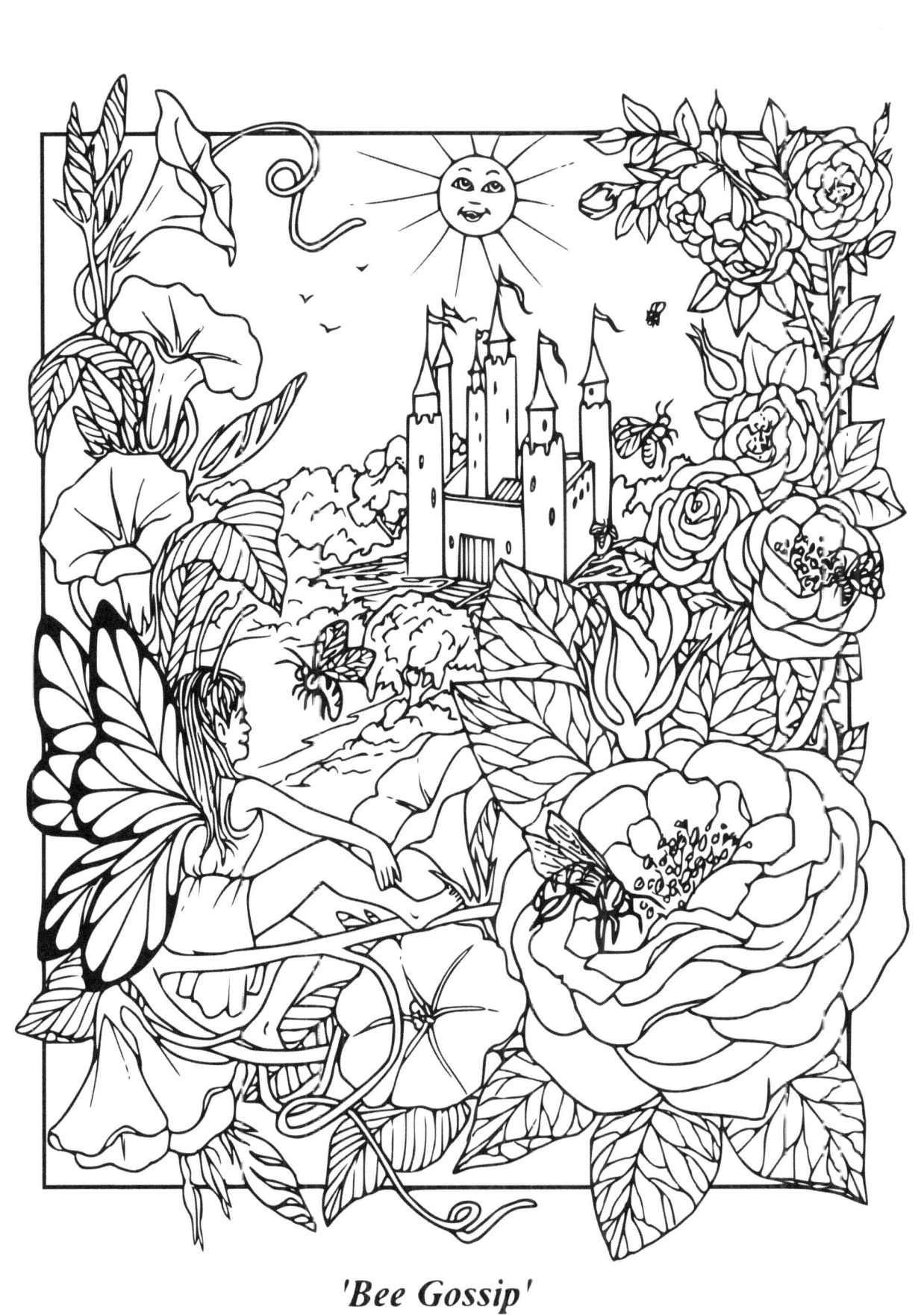

'Bee Gossip'

© Susan Curry 2018

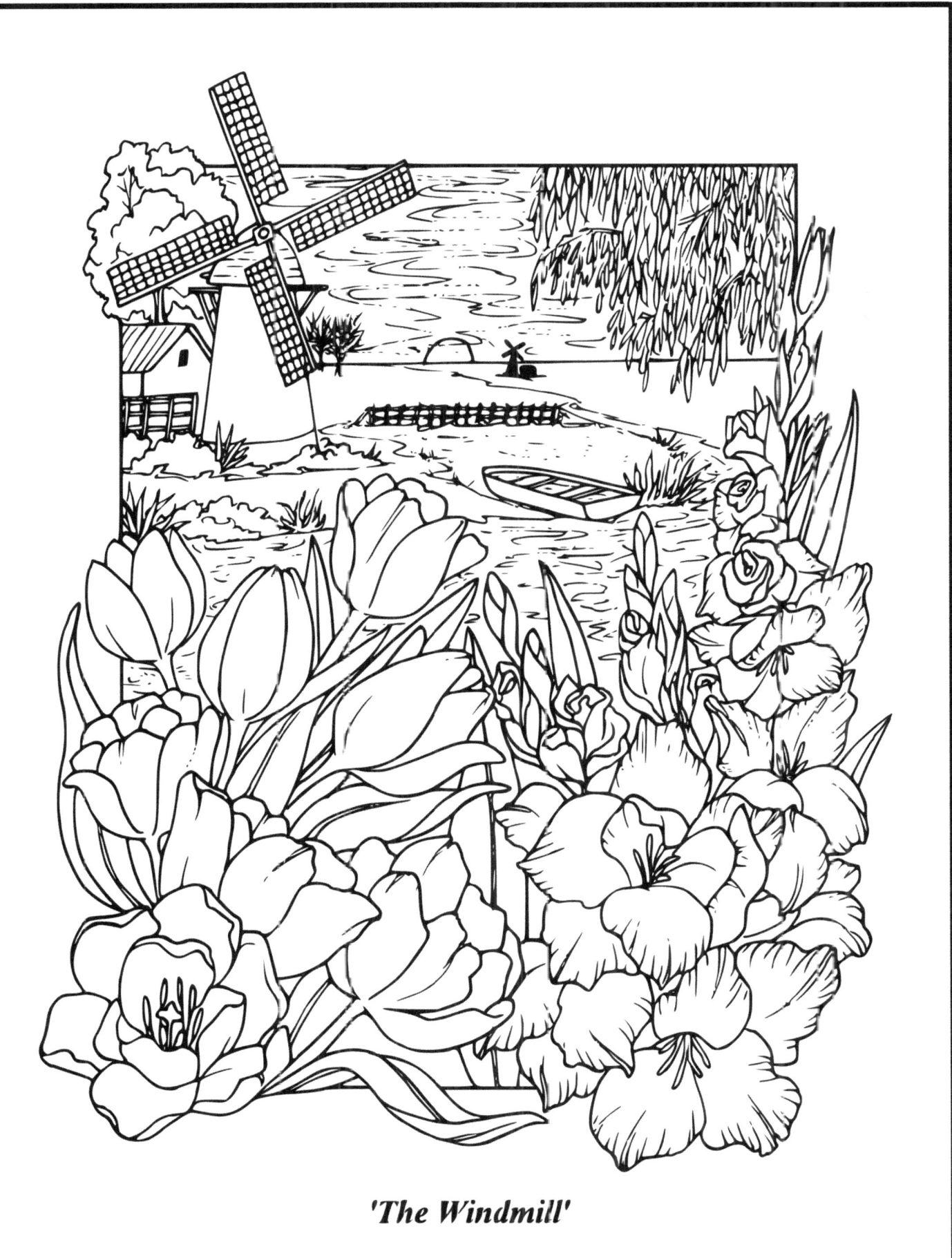

'The Windmill'

© Susan Curry 2018

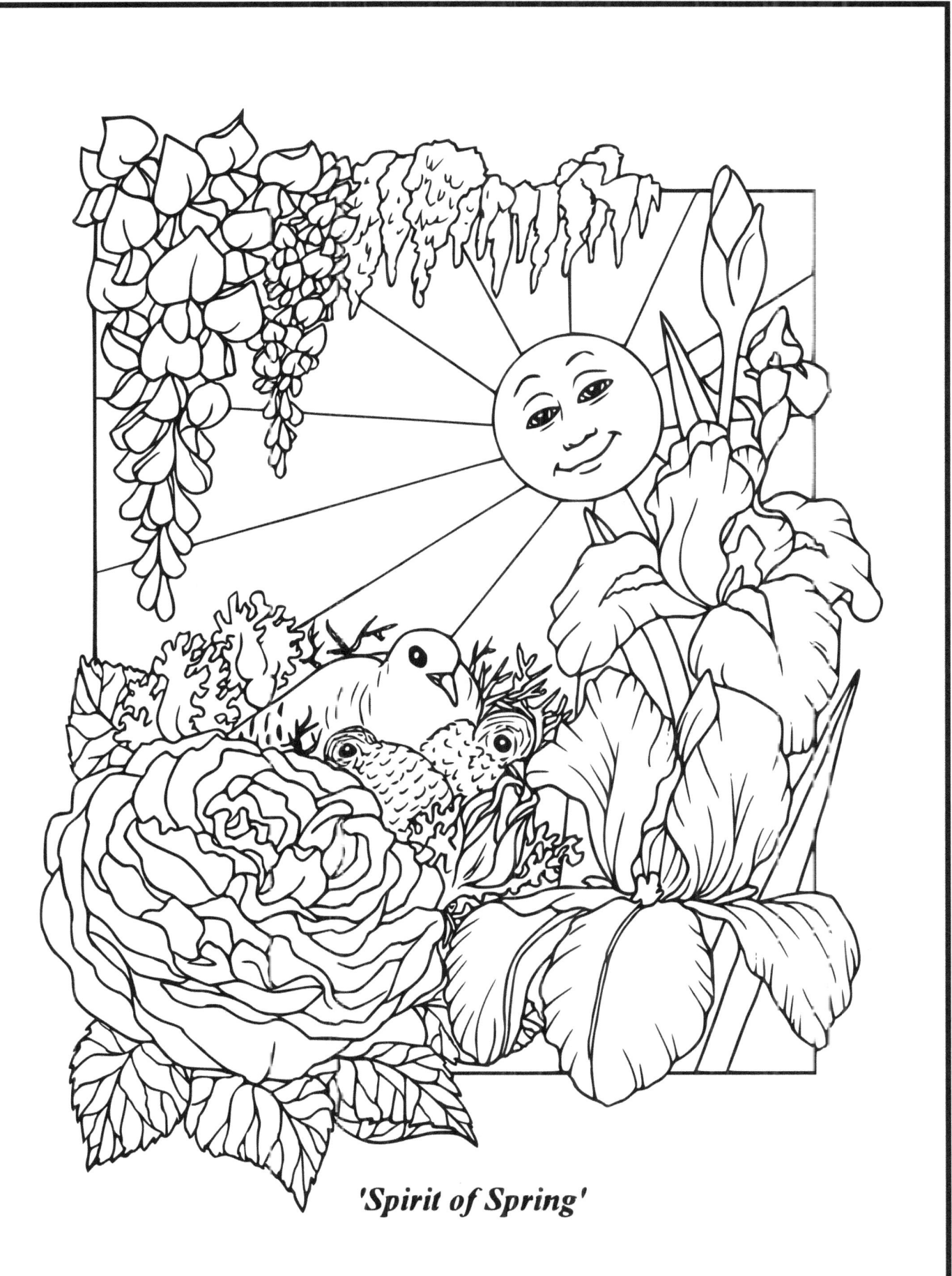

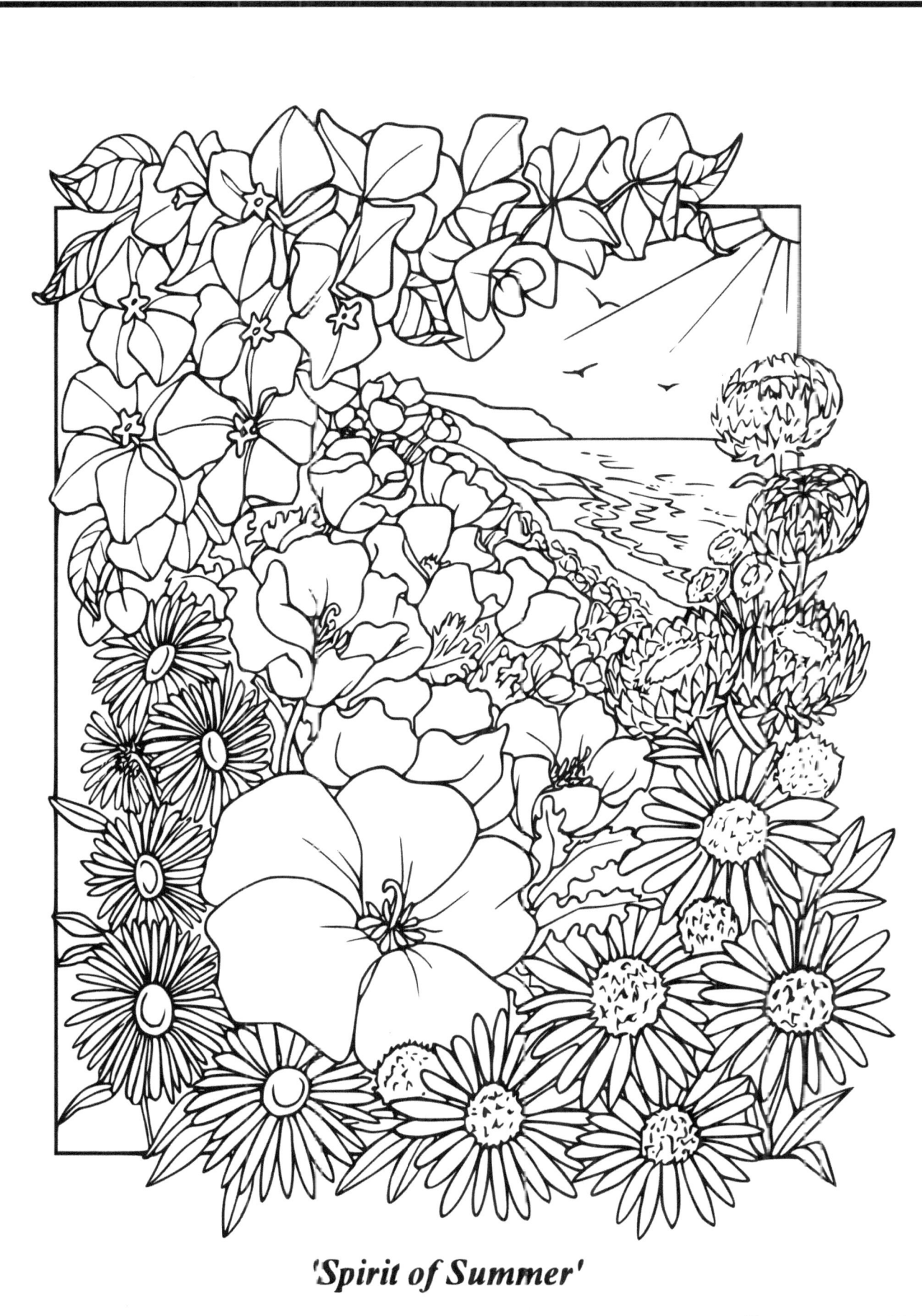
'Spirit of Summer'

© Susan Curry 2018

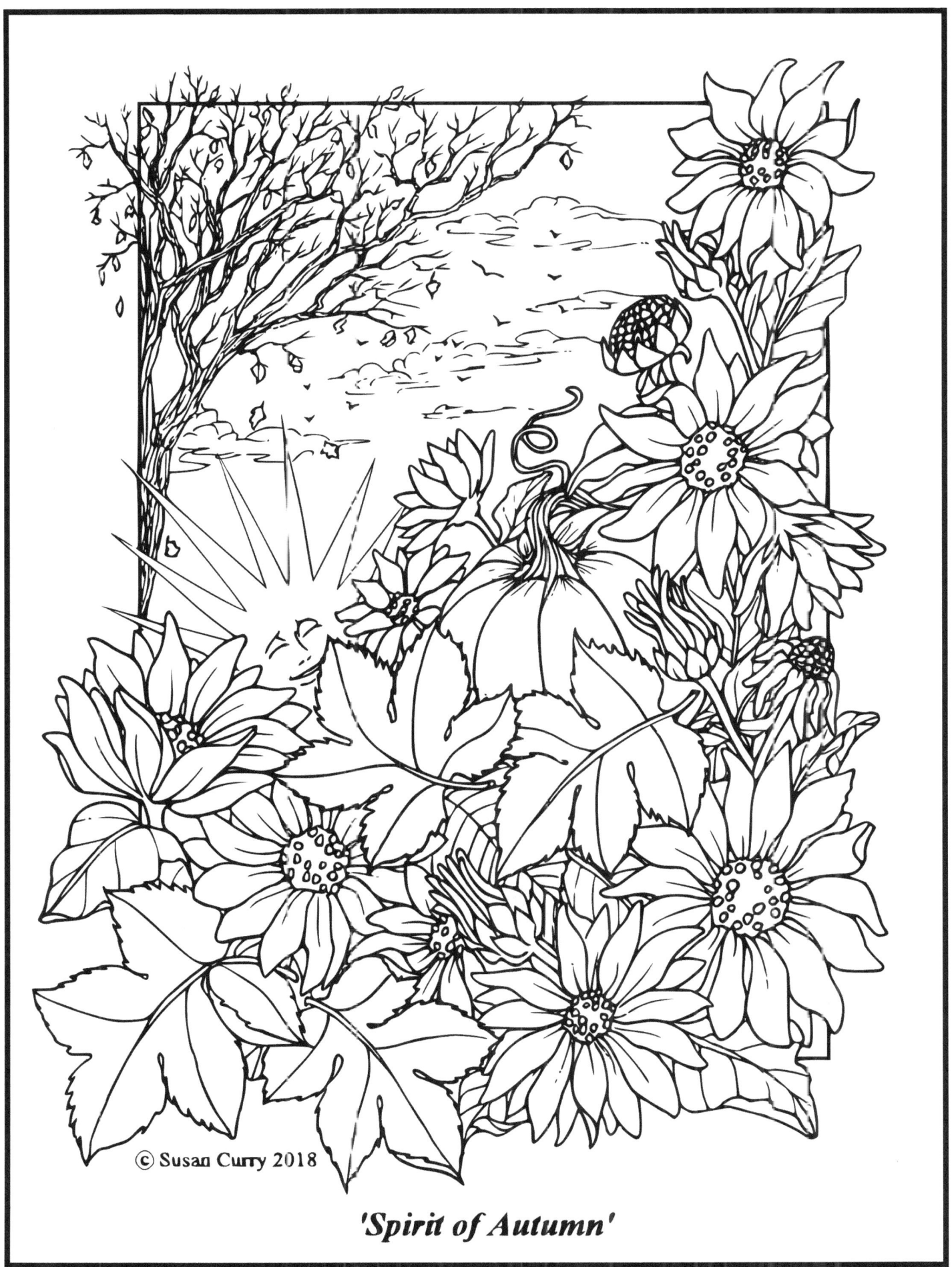

'Spirit of Autumn'

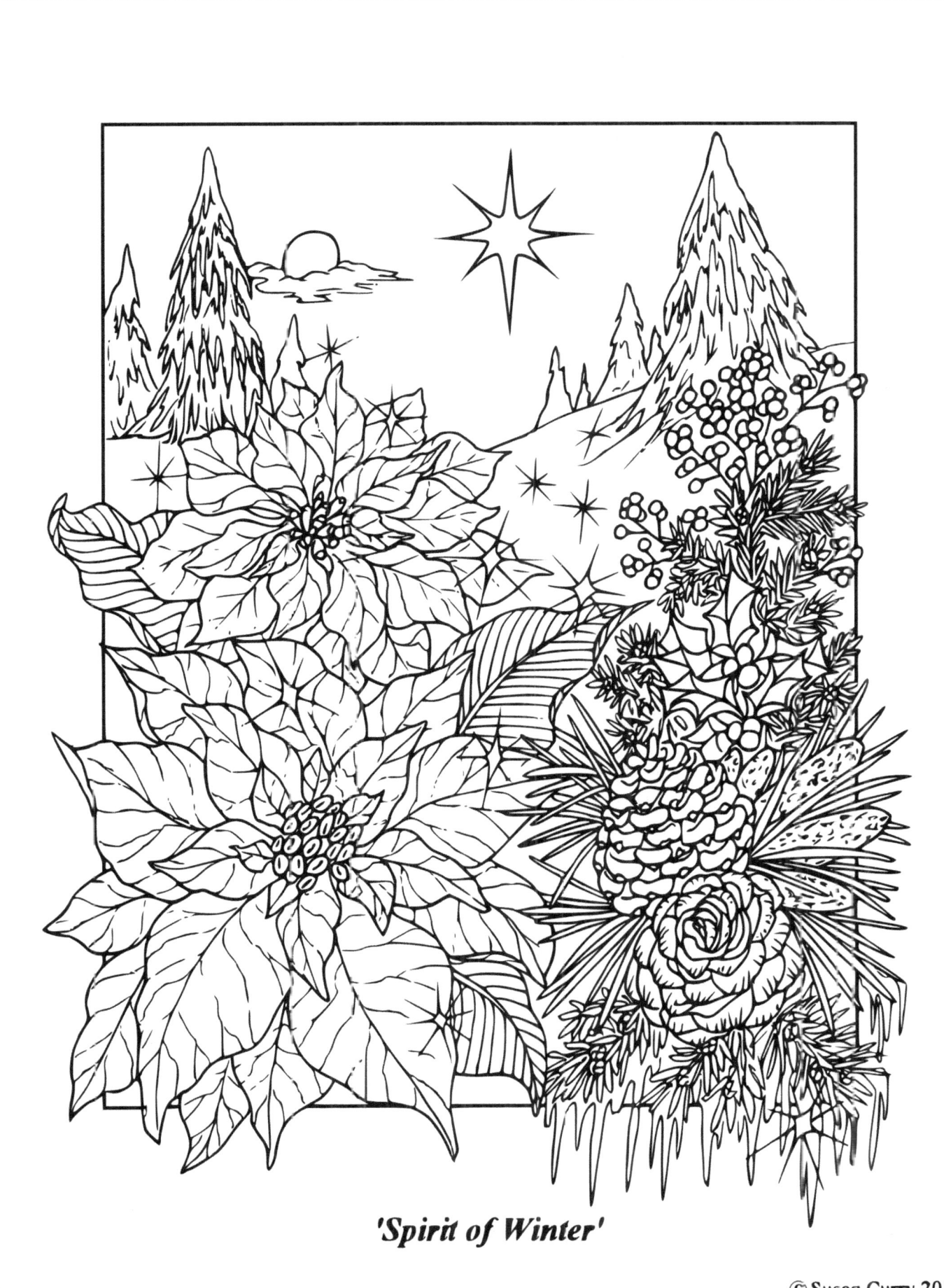

'Spirit of Winter'

© Susan Curry 2018

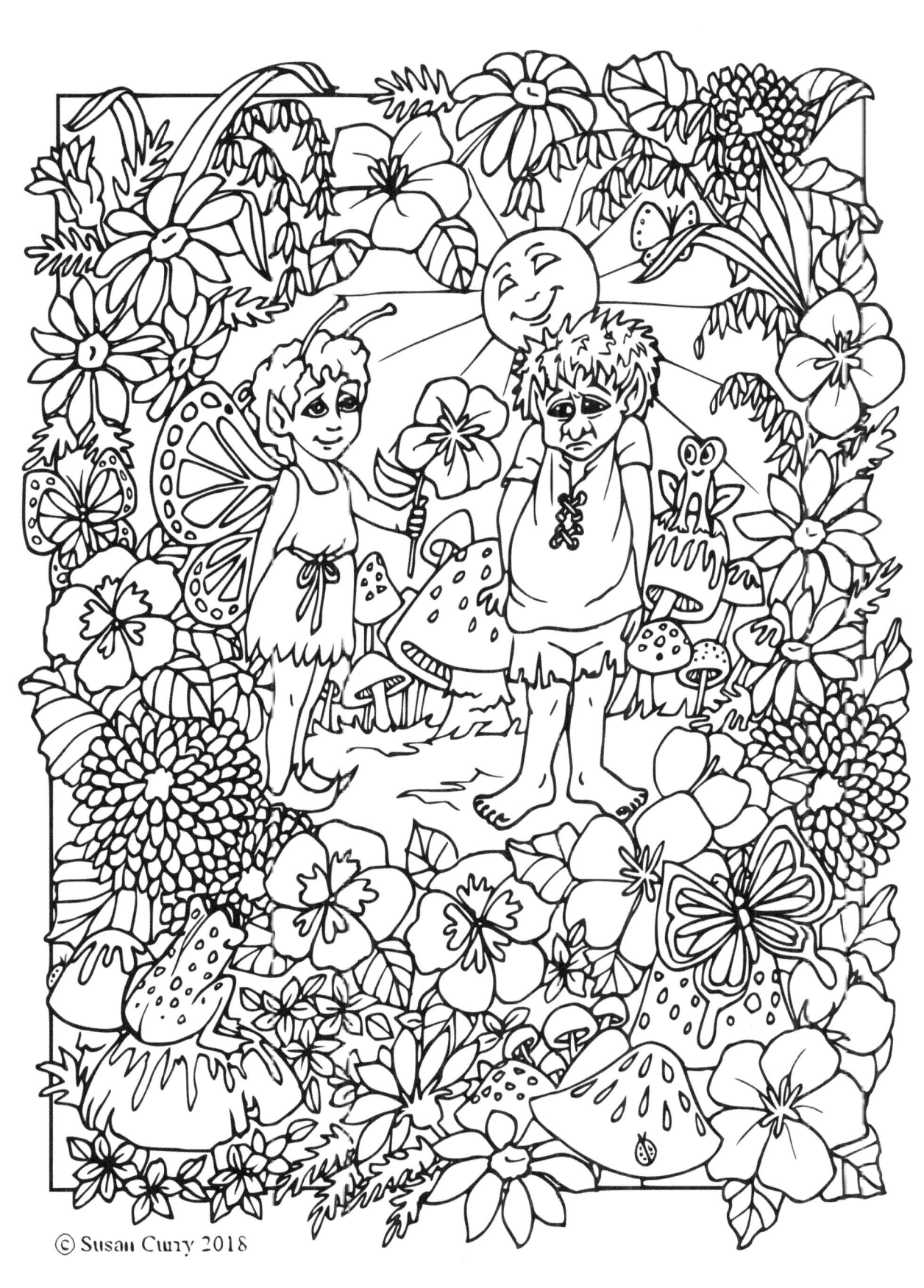

'Let's Be Friends'

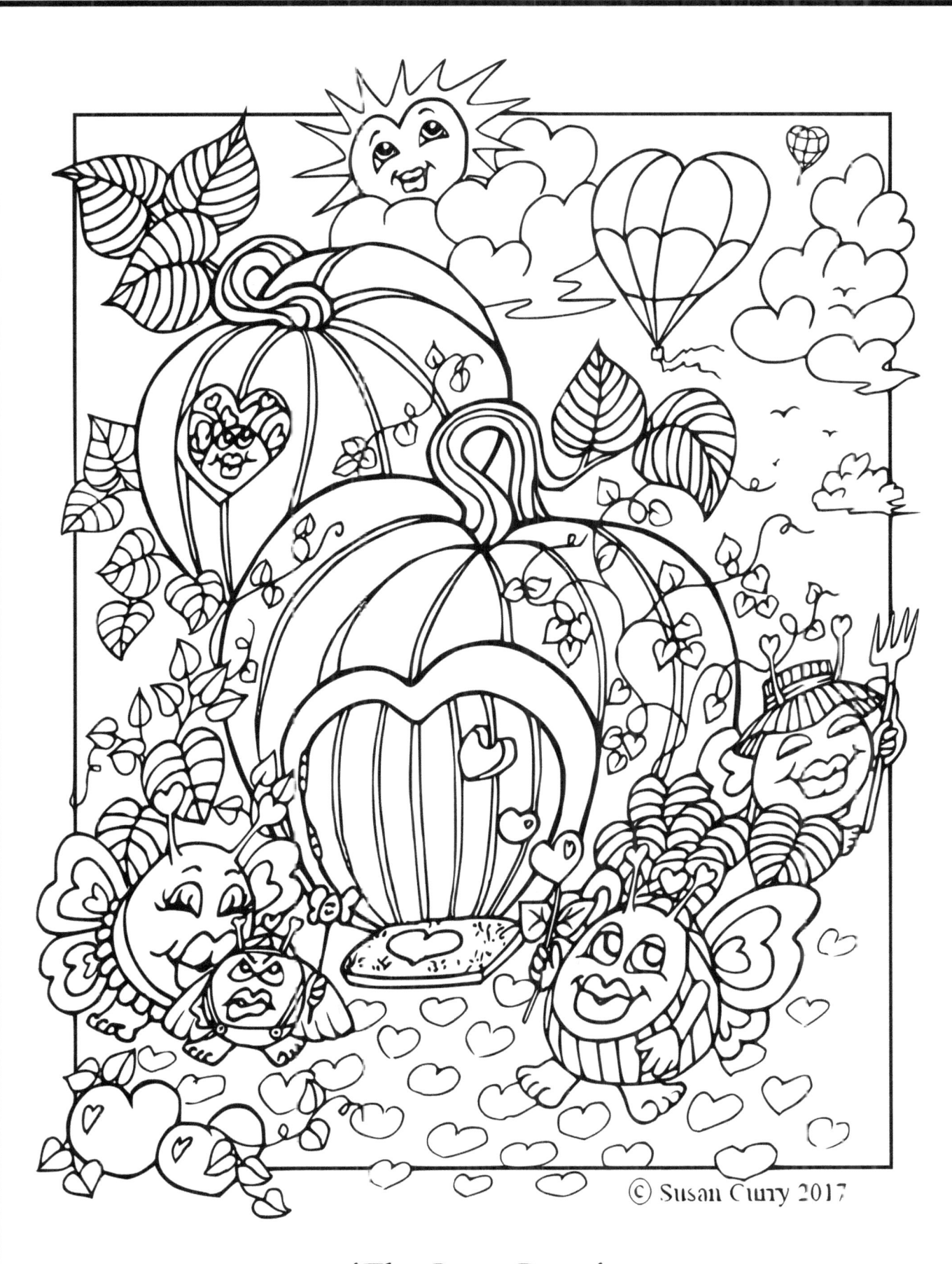

'The Love Bugs'

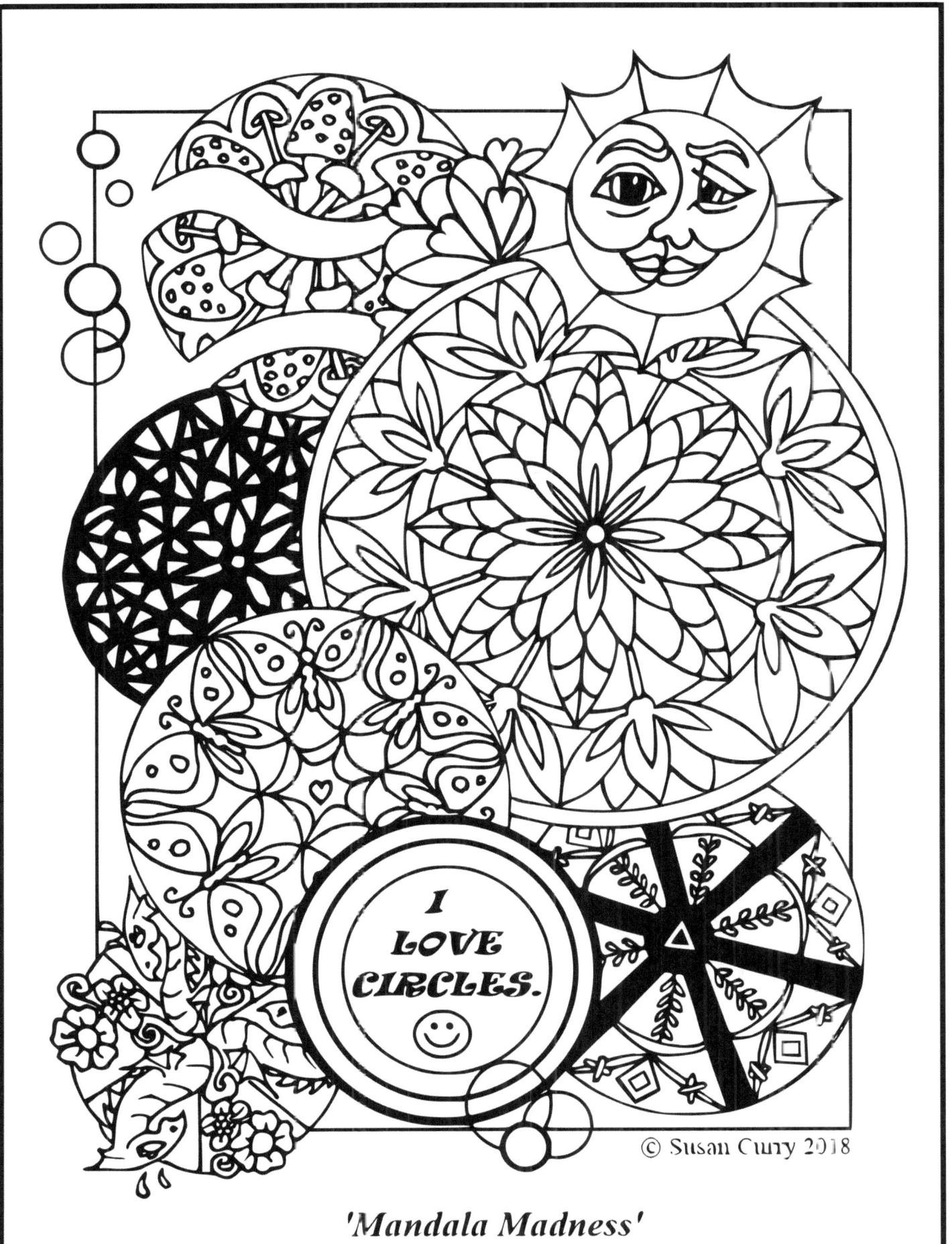

'Mandala Madness'

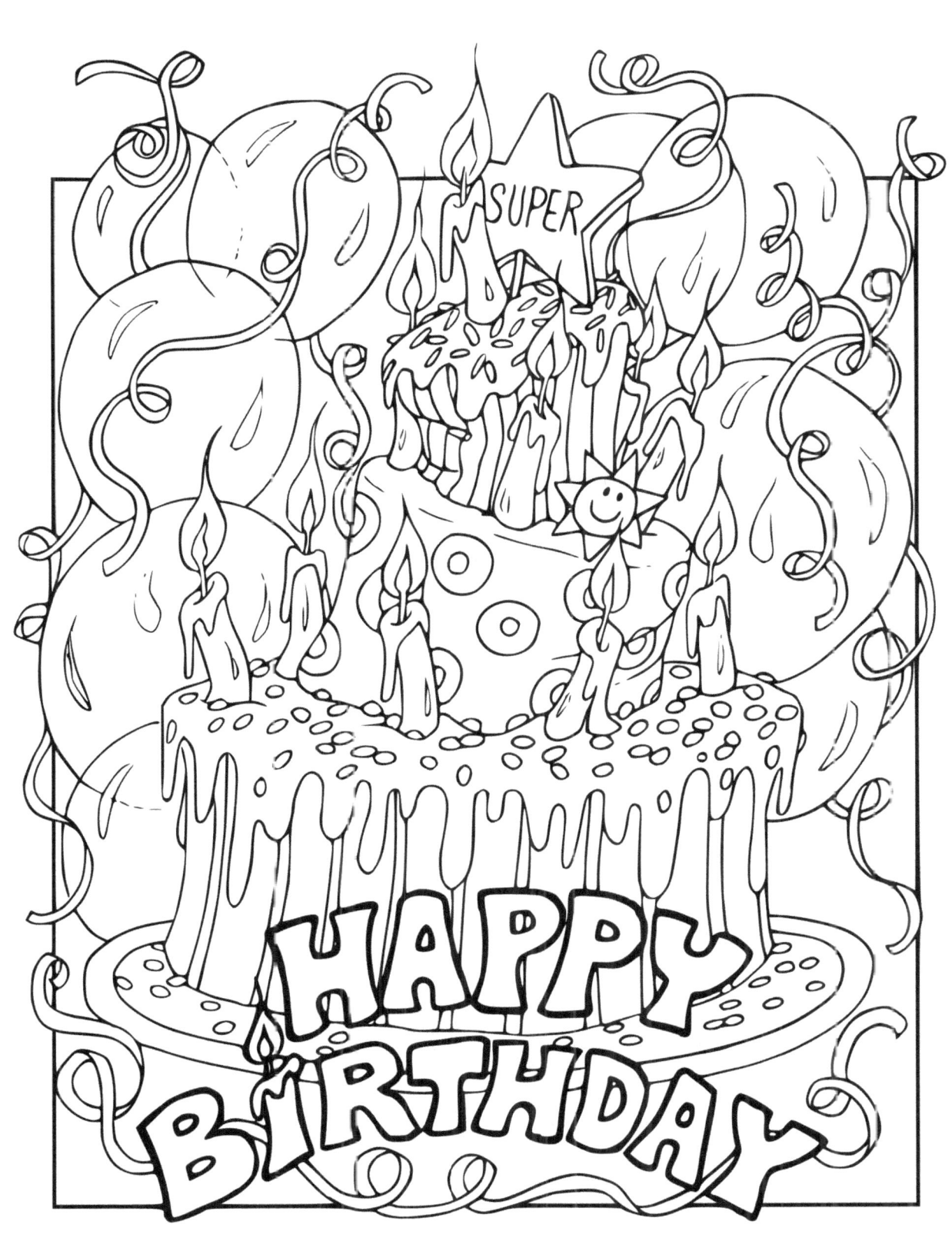

'Happy Birthday'

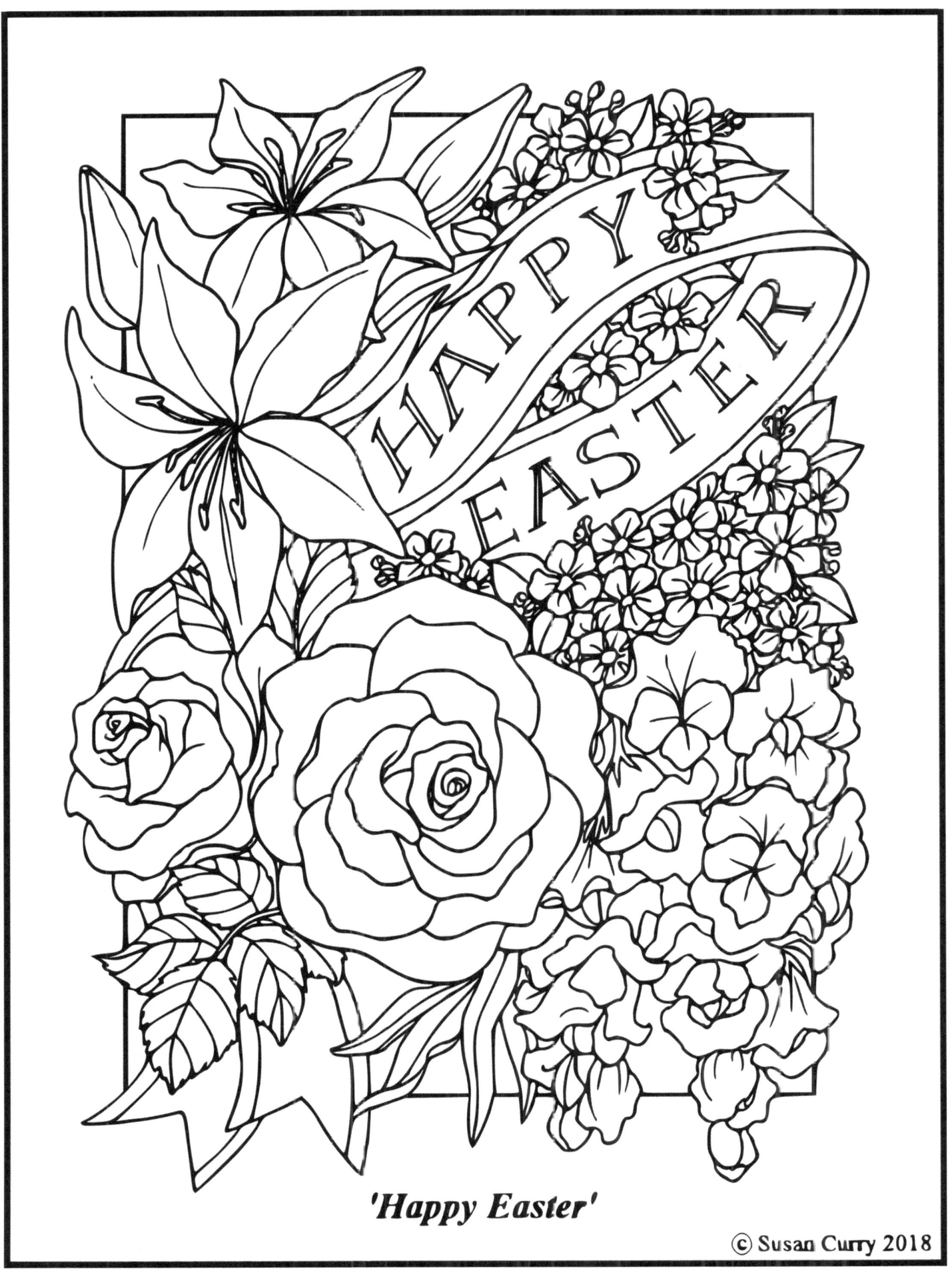

'Happy Easter'

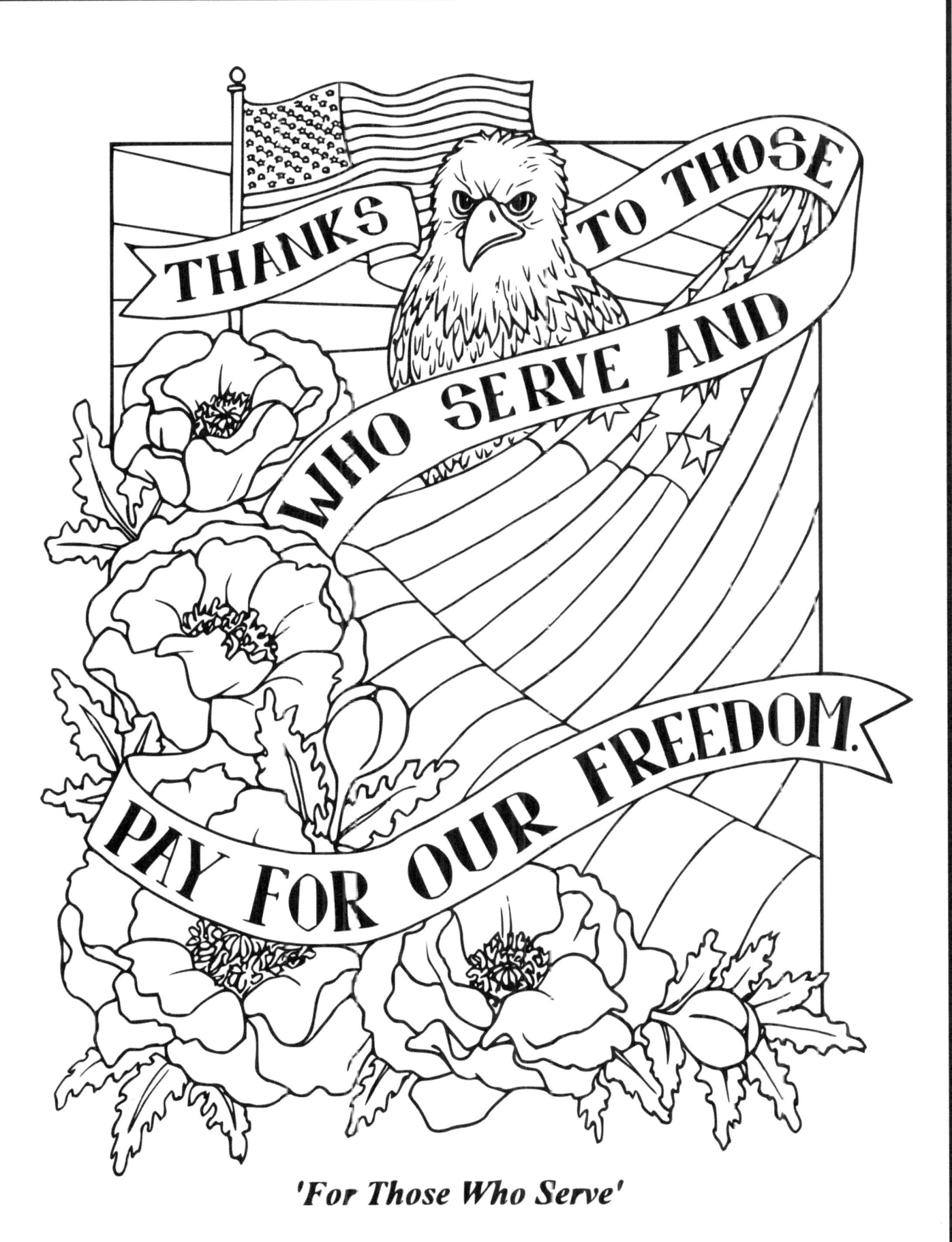

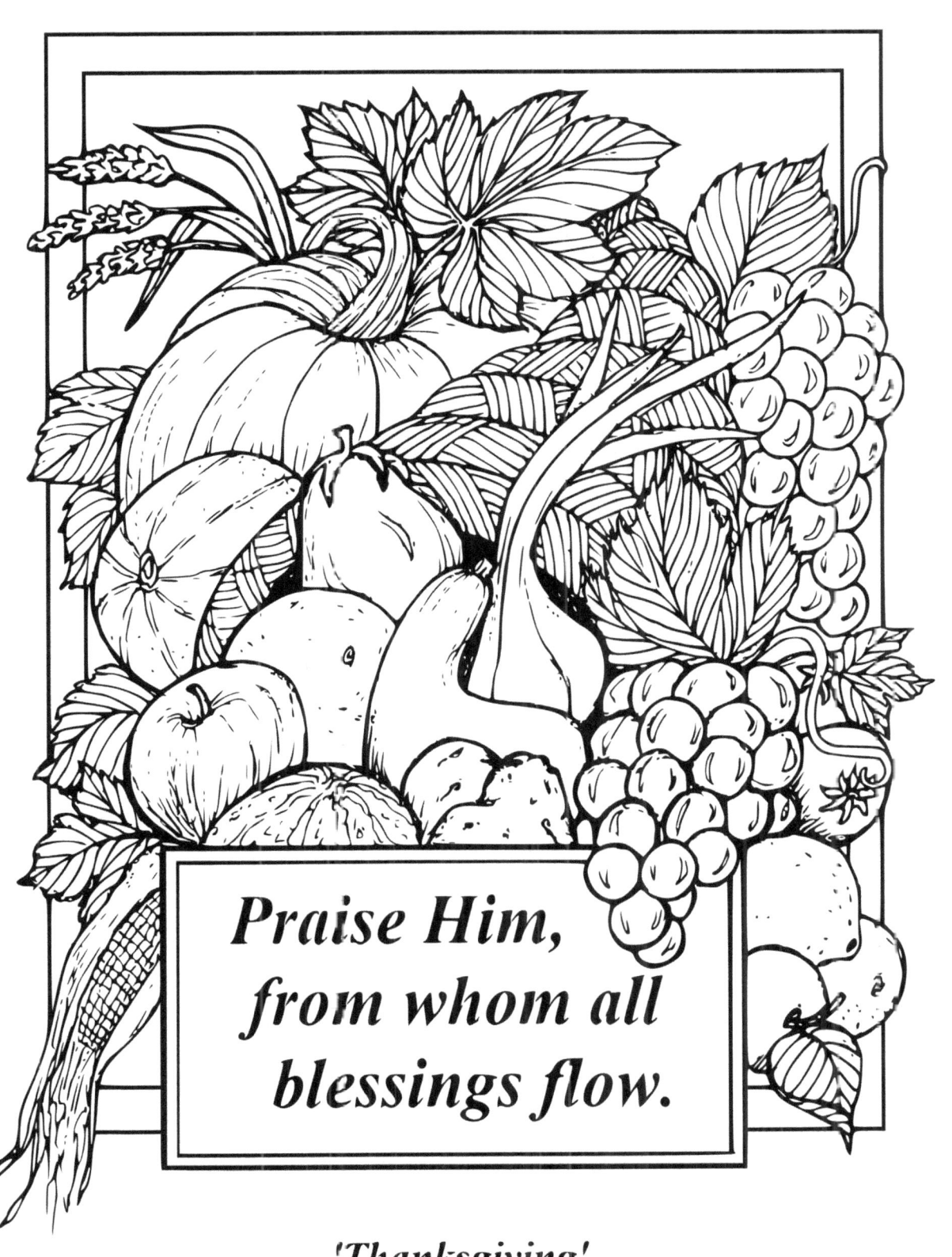

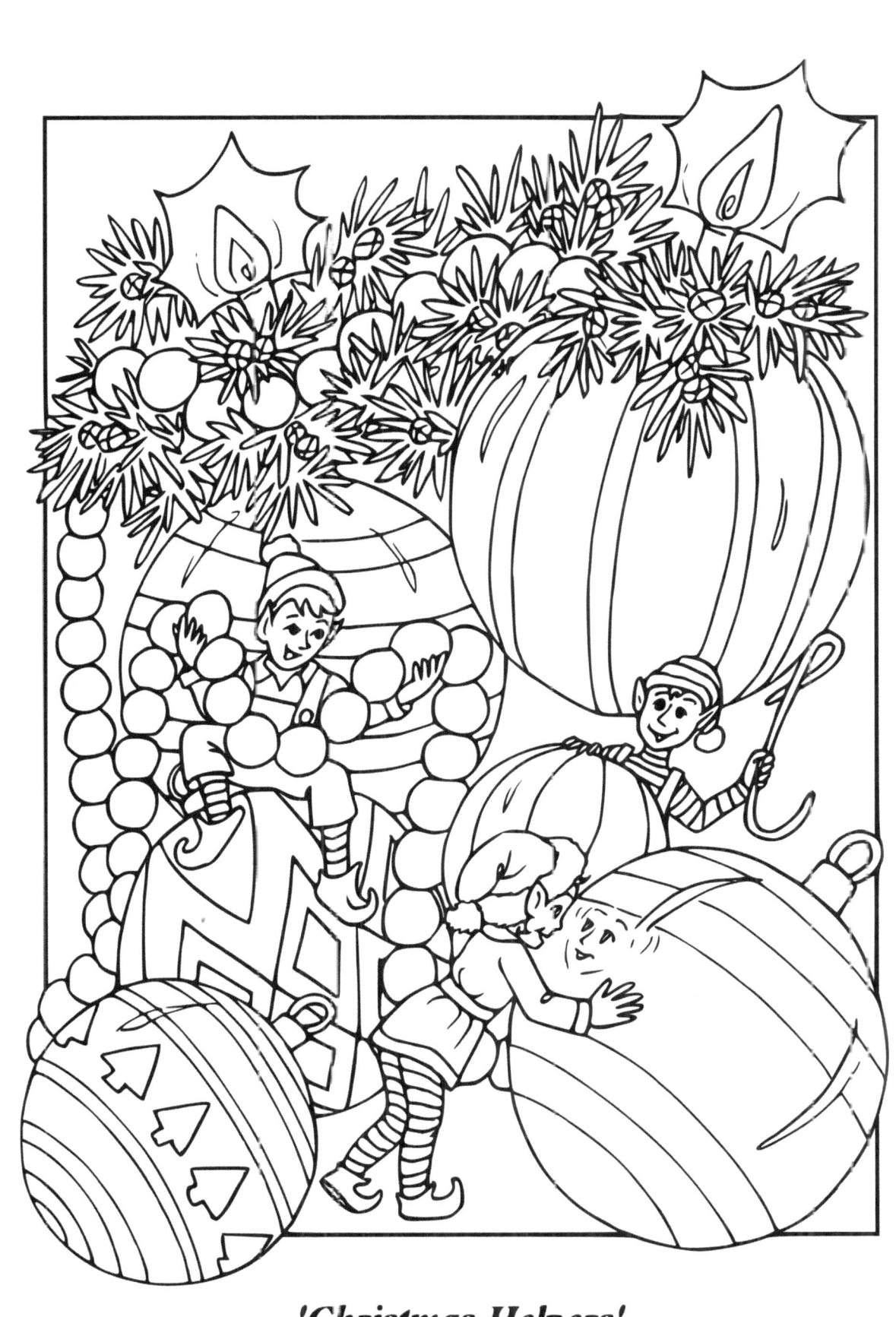

'Christmas Helpers'

© Susan Curry 2018

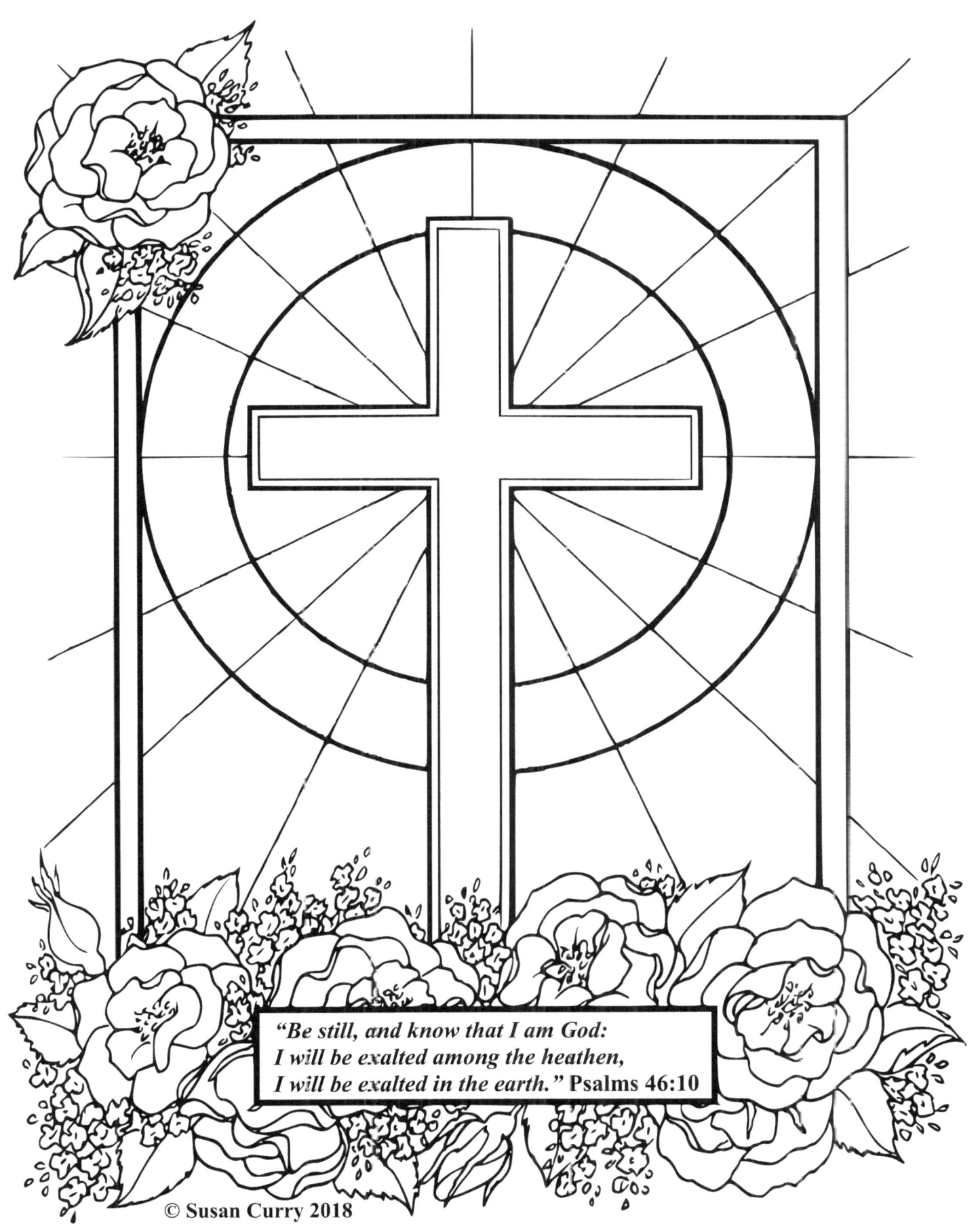

'Be Still and Know'

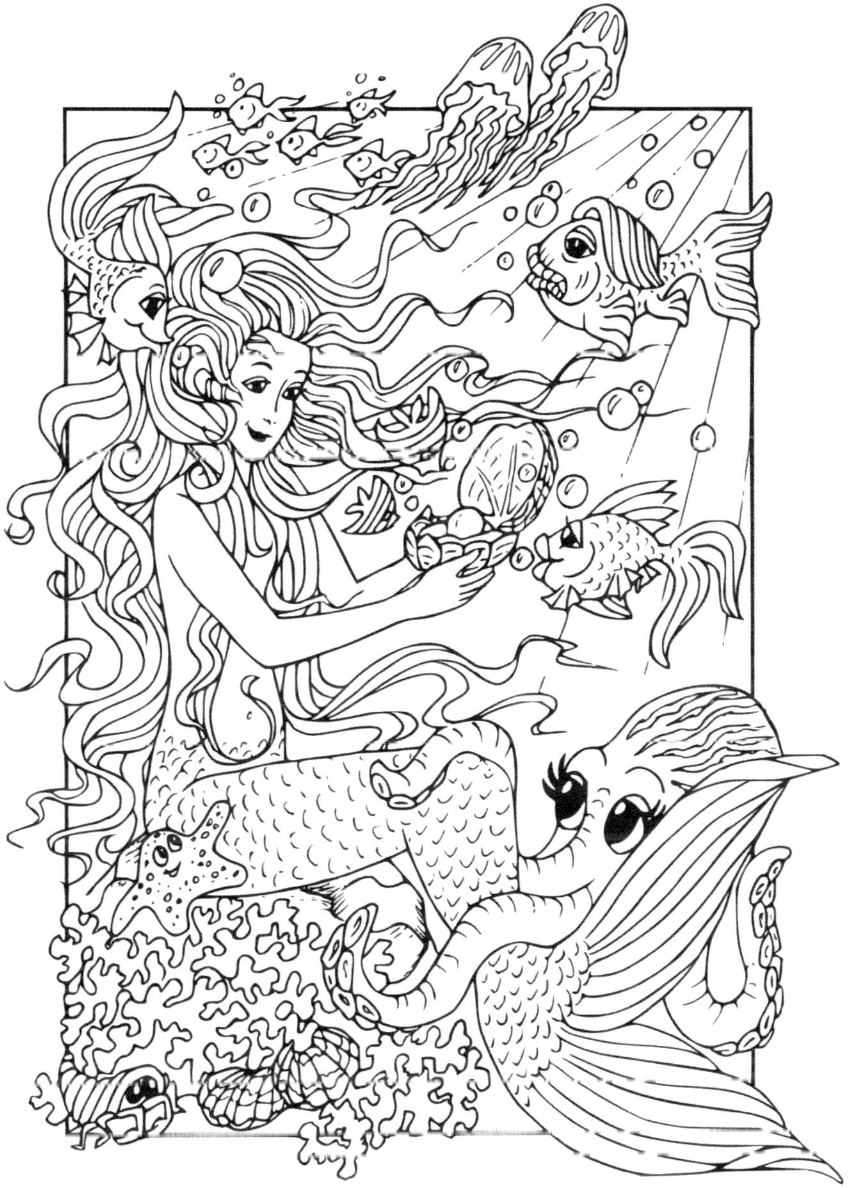

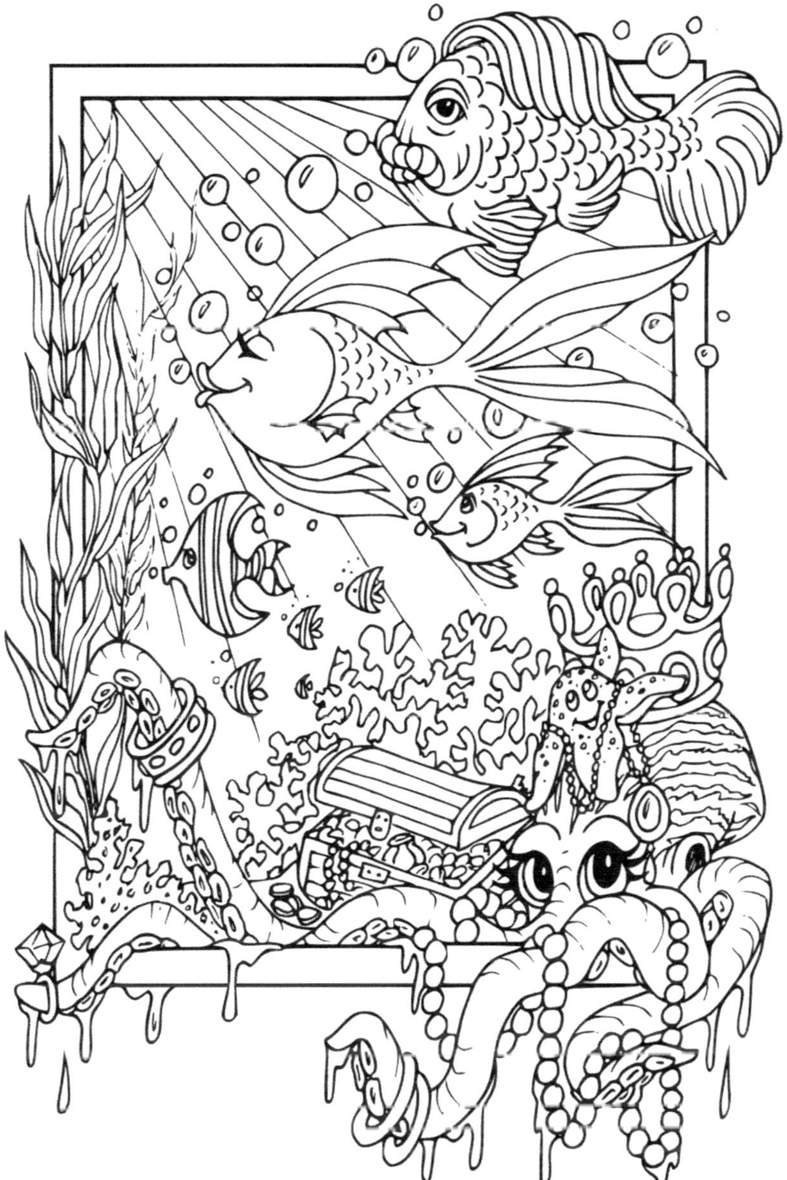

'Finders Keepers' © Susan Curry 2018

'The Pearl' © Susan Curry 2018

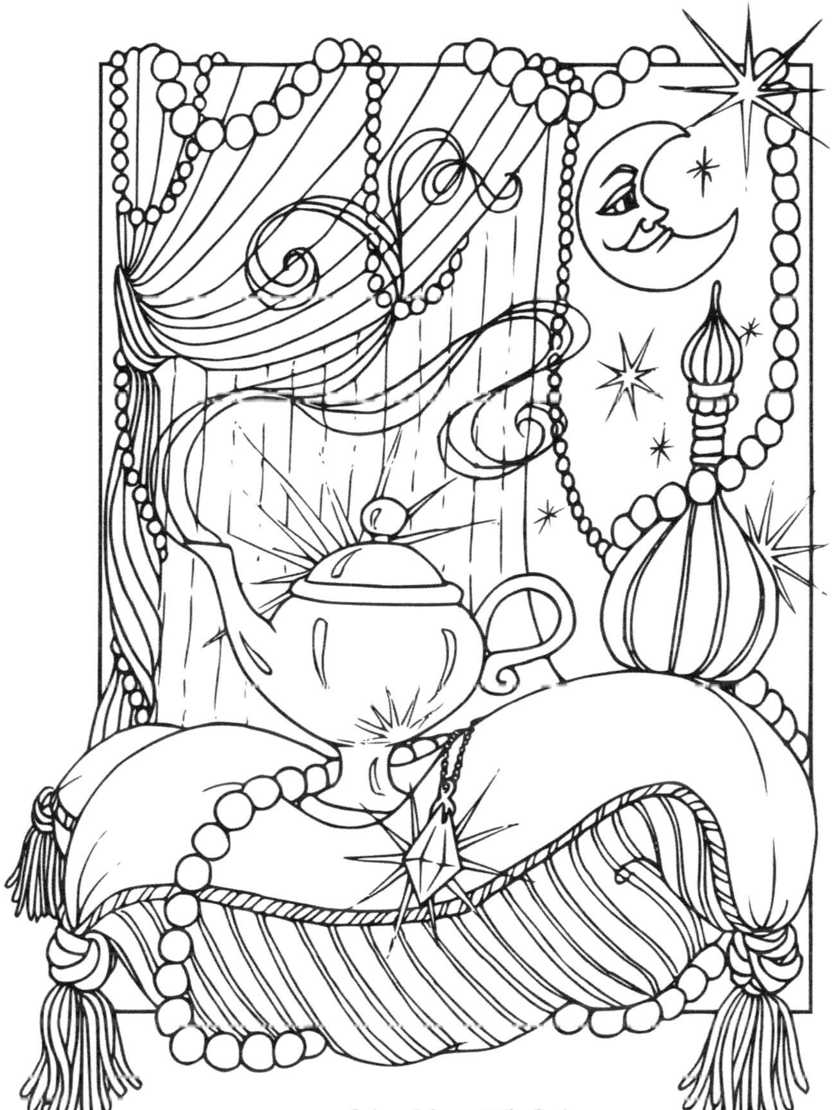

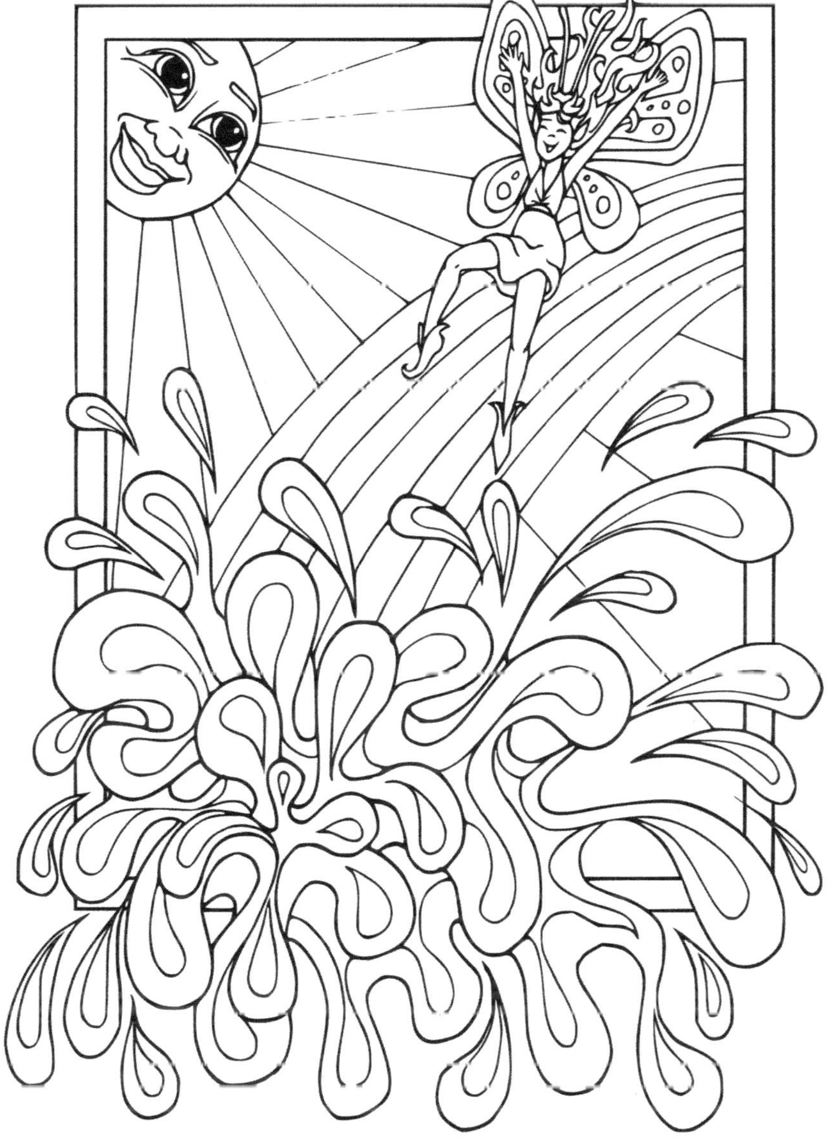

'Rainbow Splash'
© Susan Curry 2018

'Arabian Night'
© Susan Curry 2018

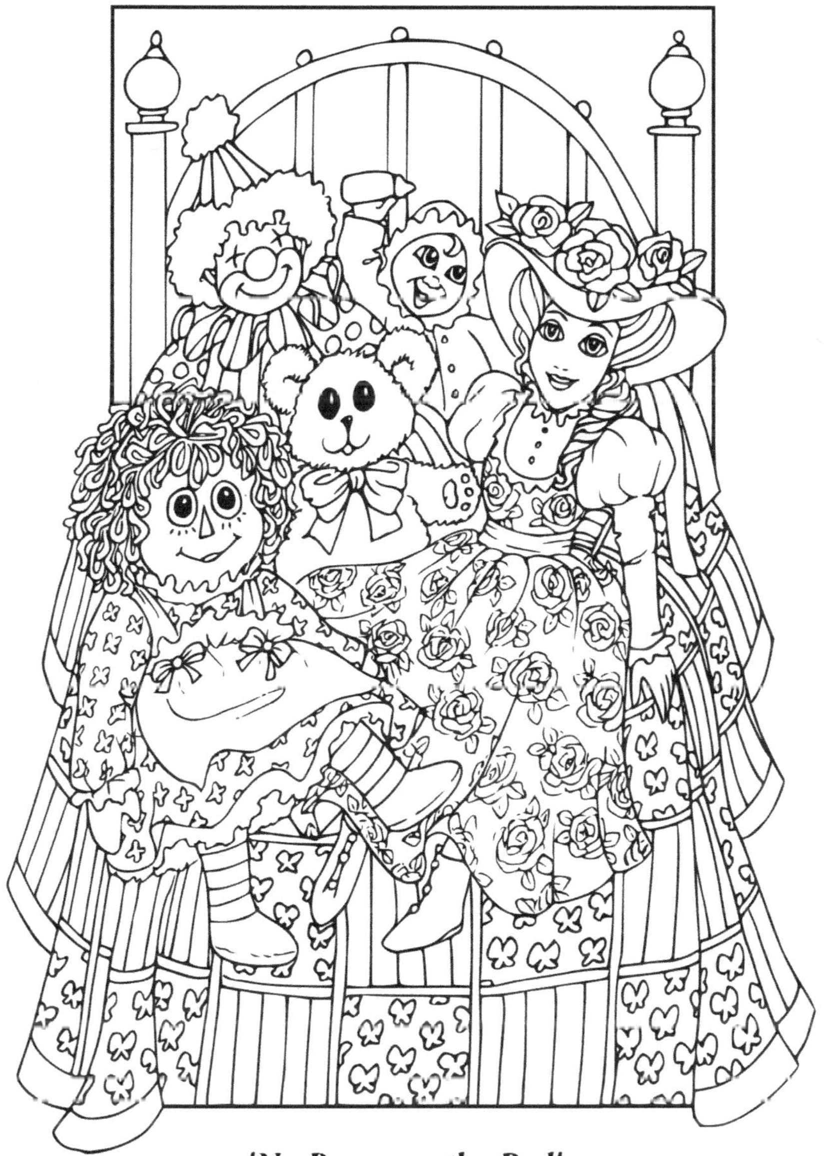

'Pop Goes The Weasel'

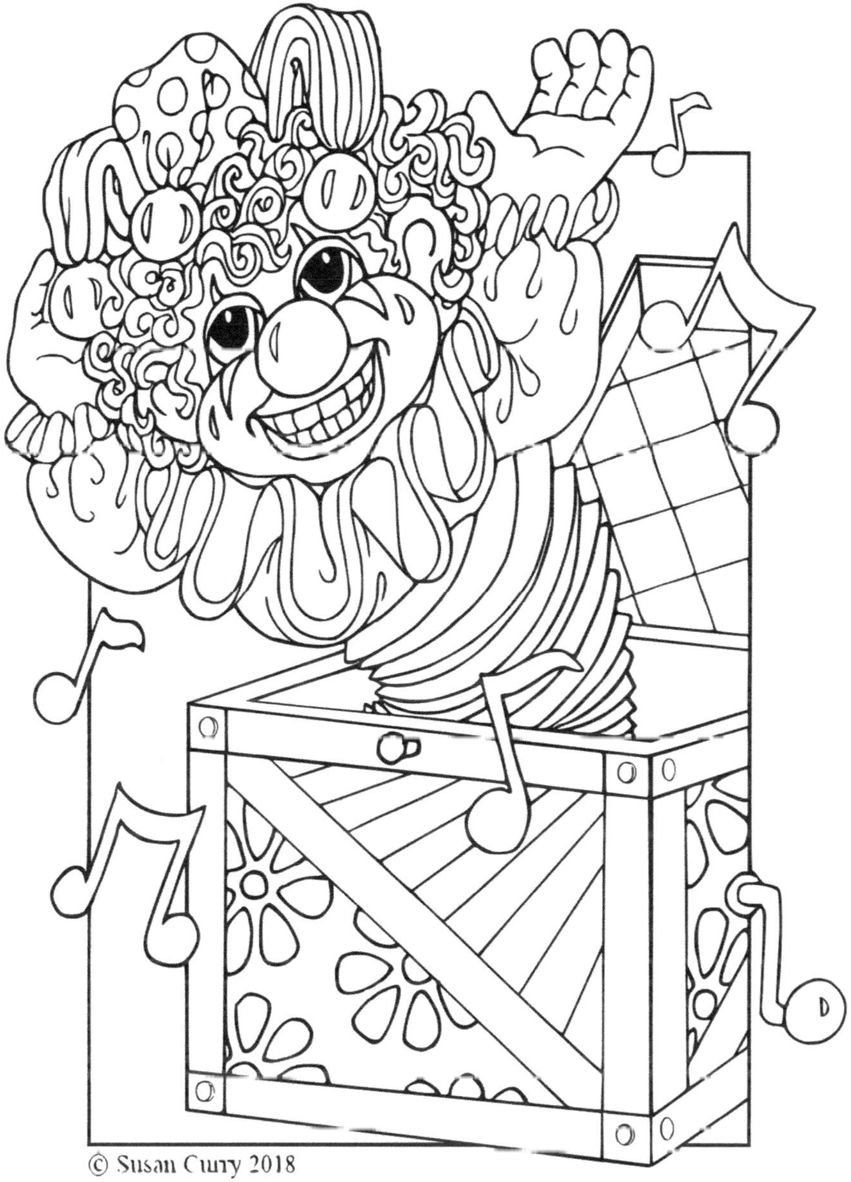

'No Room on the Bed'

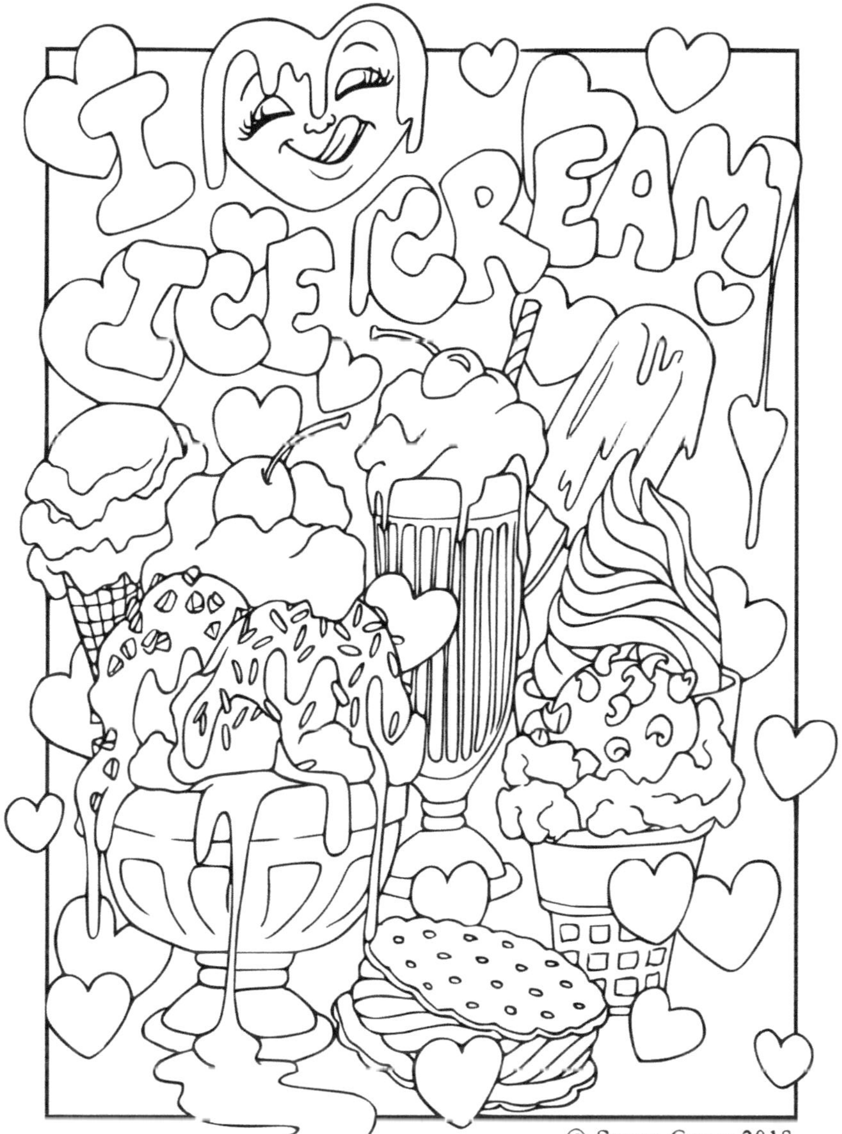

'Rose Sale'

'I Love Ice Cream'

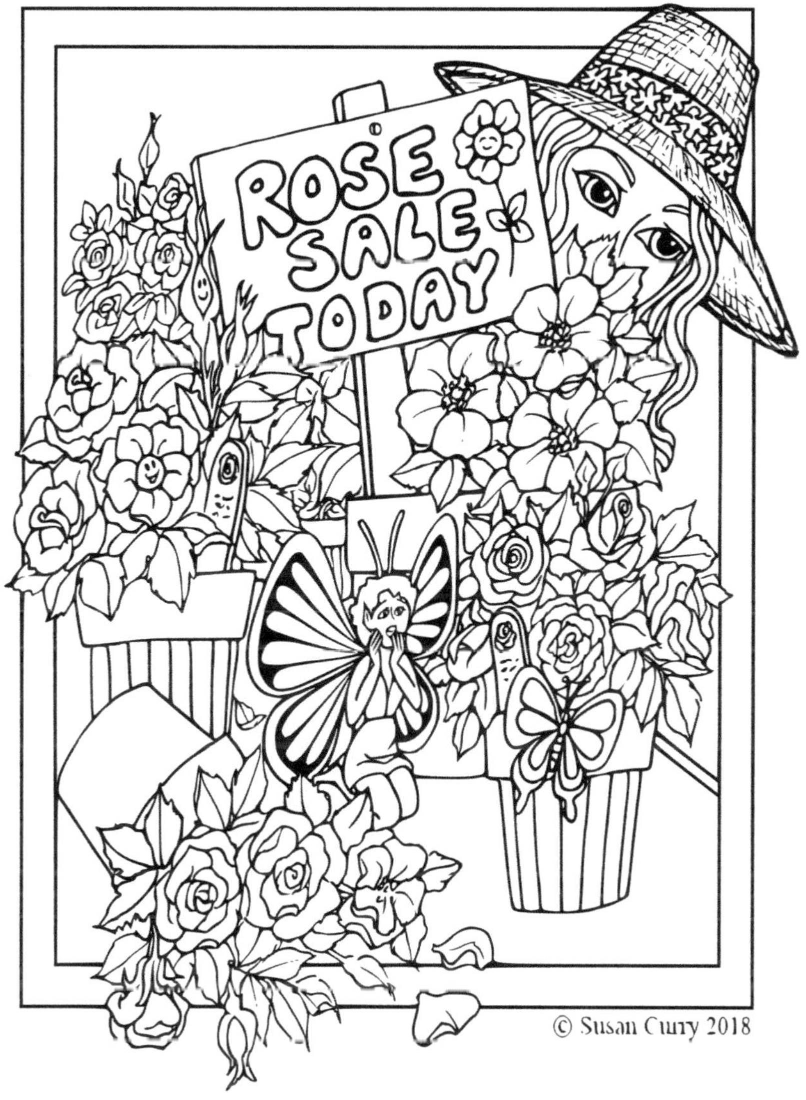

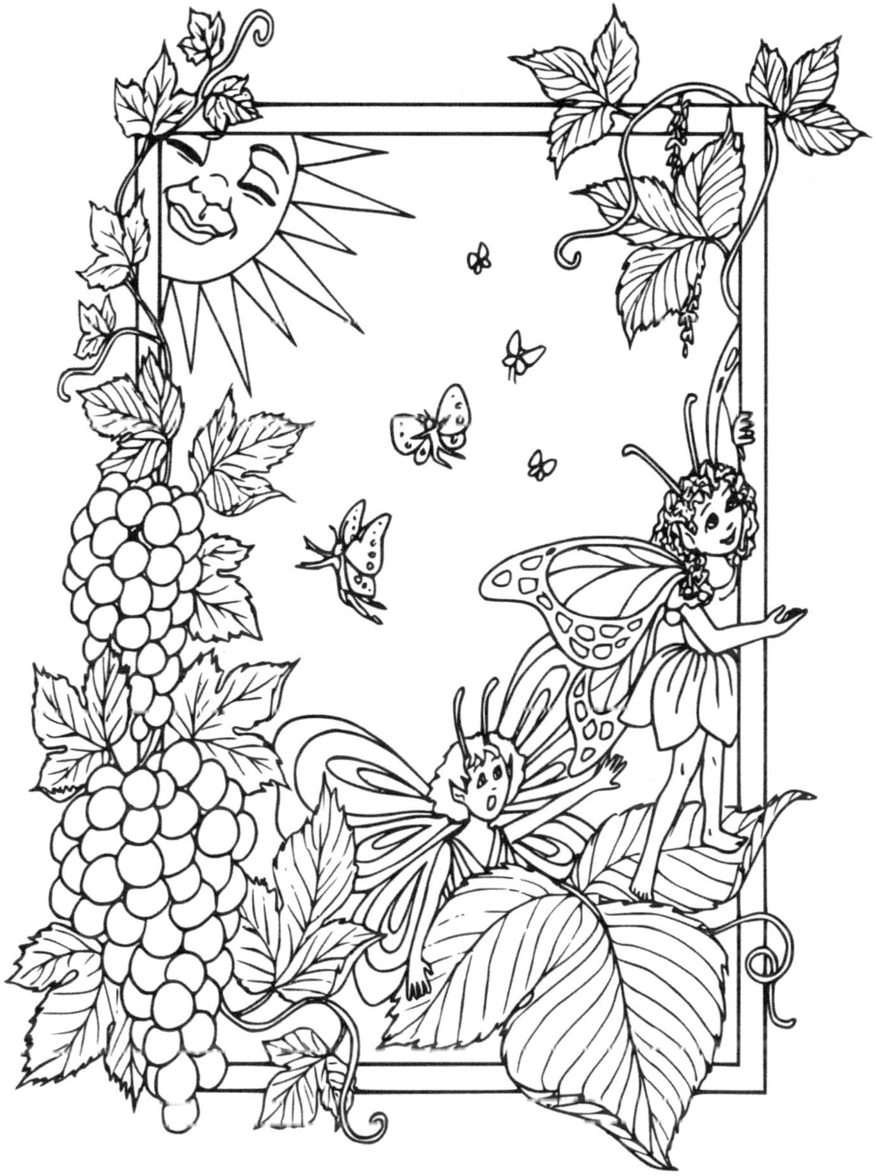

'Curiosity'

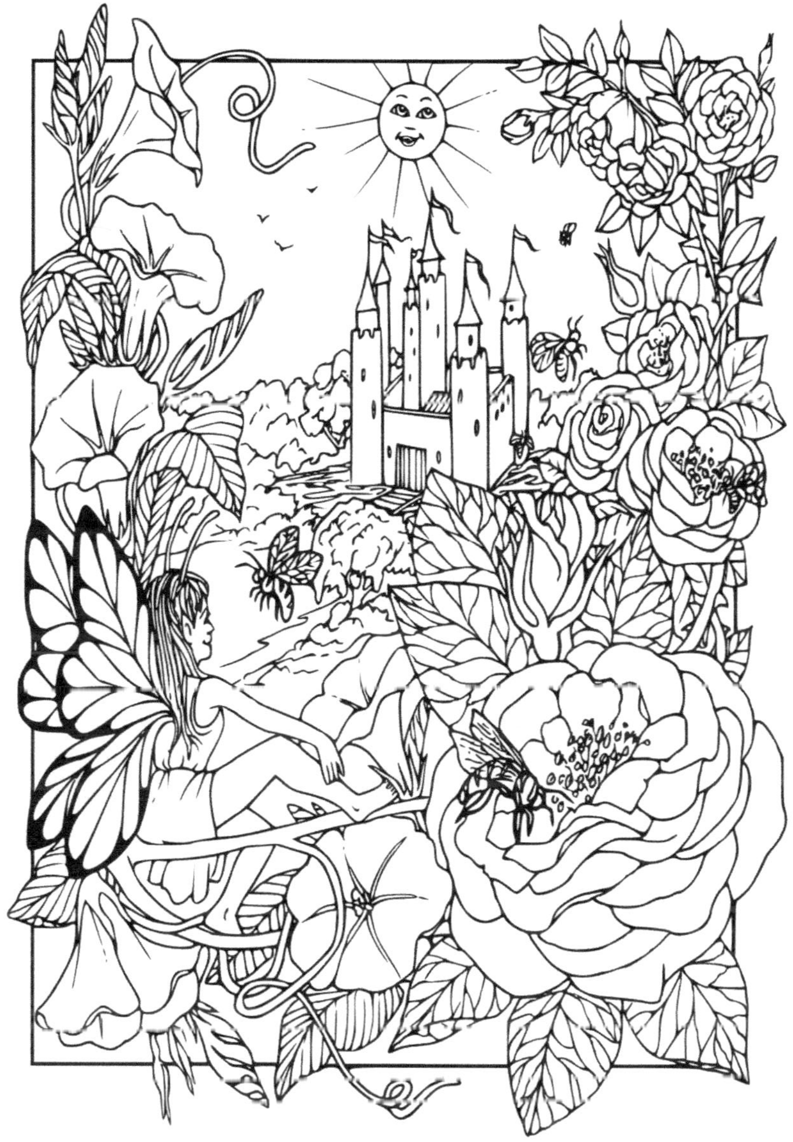

'Bee Gossip'

© Susan Curry 2018

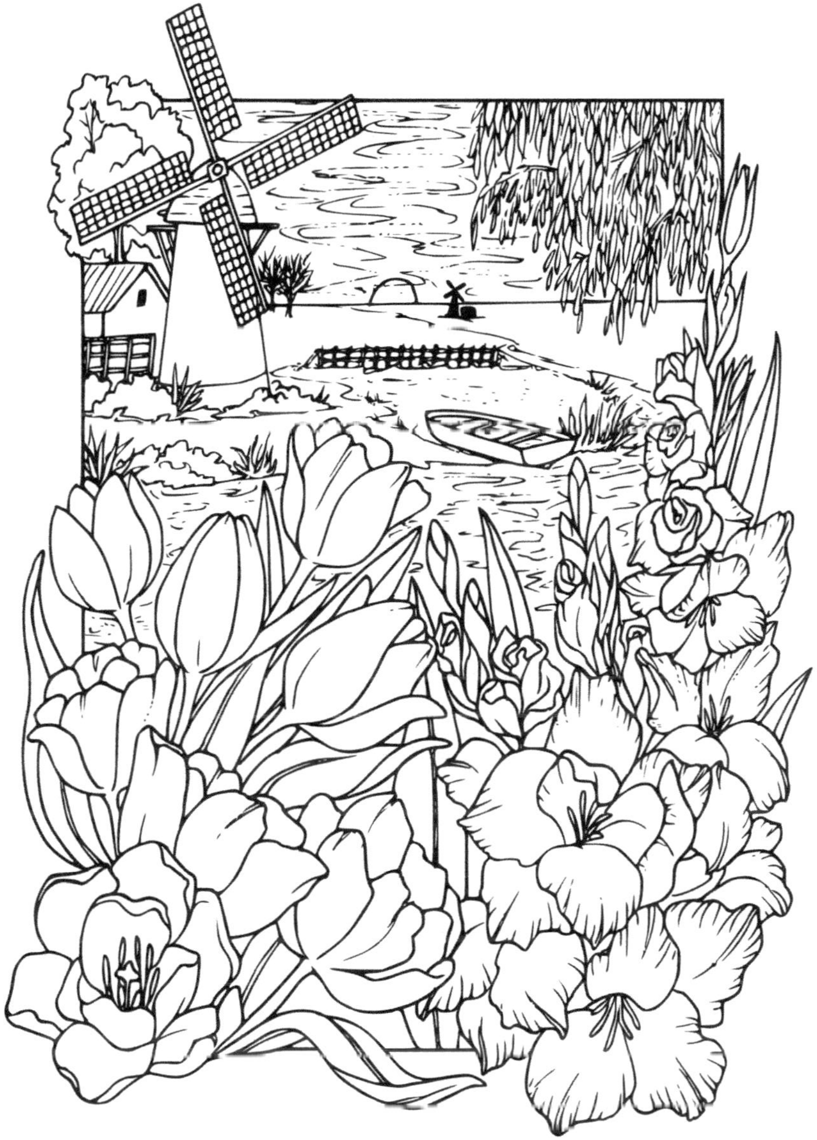

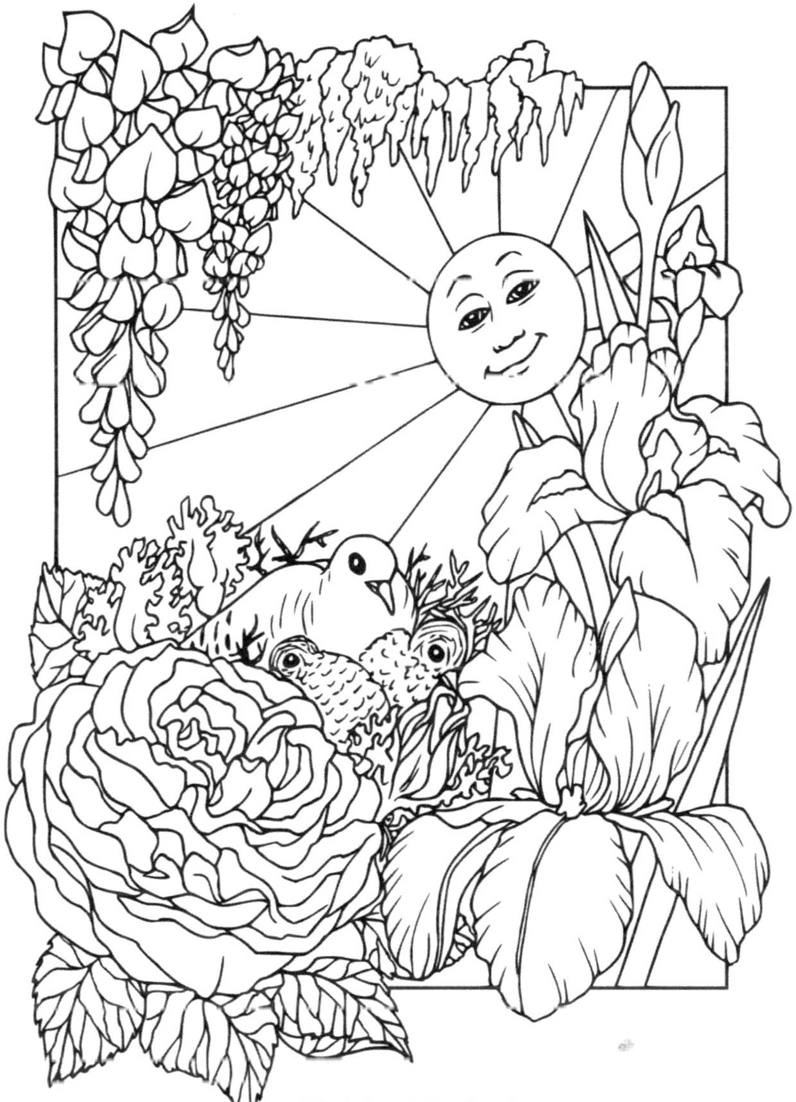

'Spirit of Spring'

© Susan Curry 2018

'The Windmill'

© Susan Curry 2018

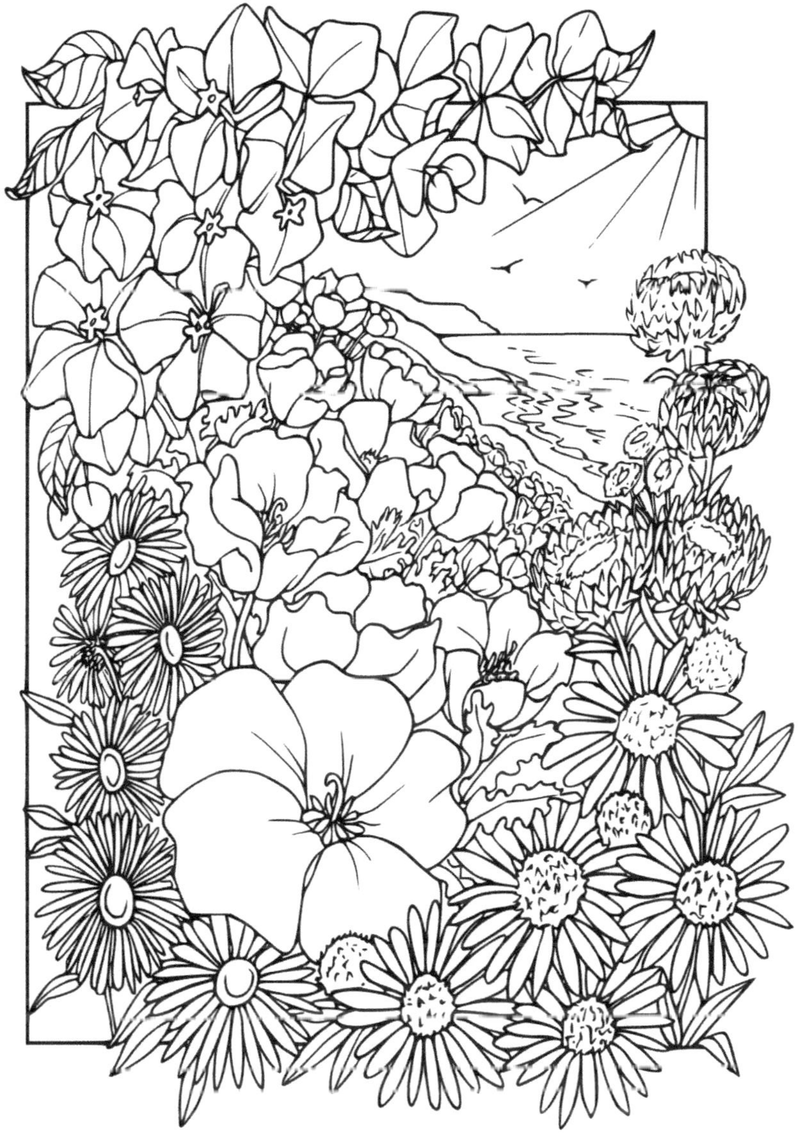

'Spirit of Autumn'
© Susan Curry 2018

'Spirit of Summer'
© Susan Curry 2018

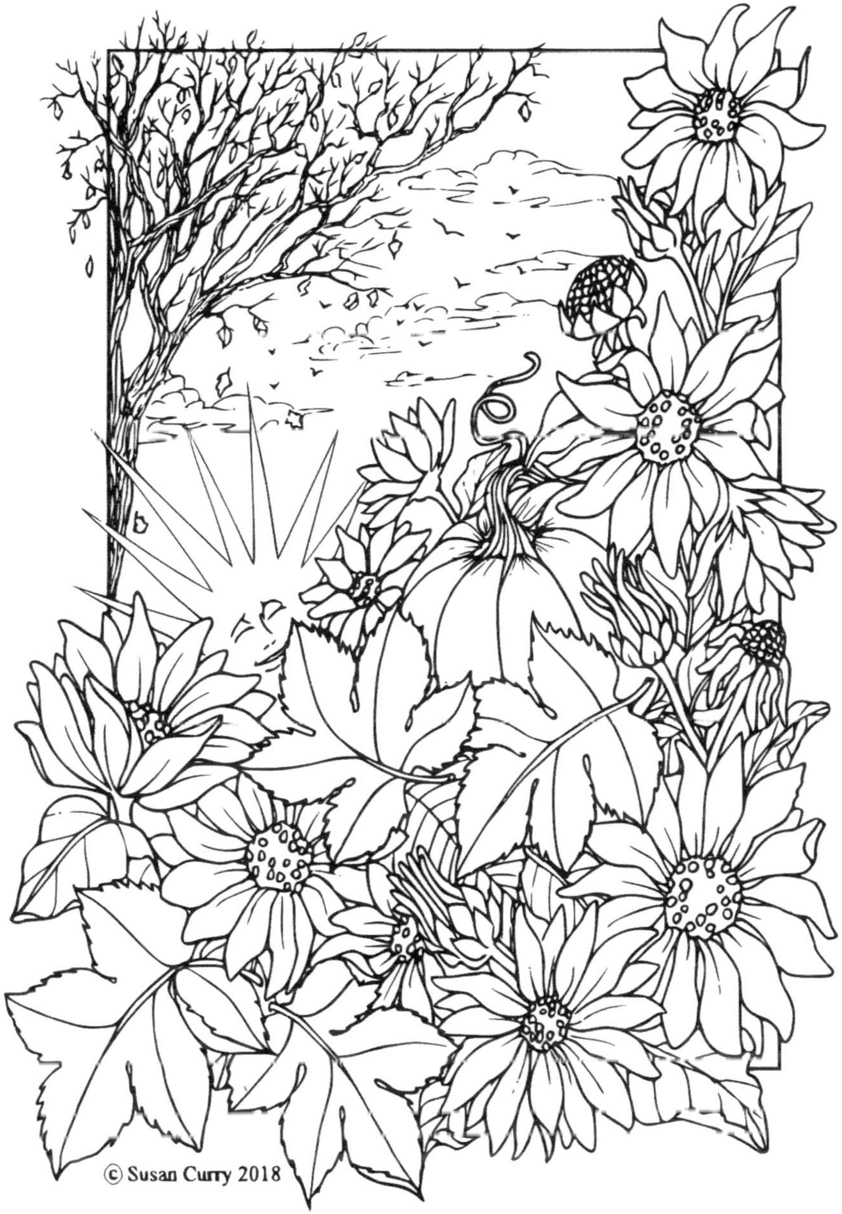

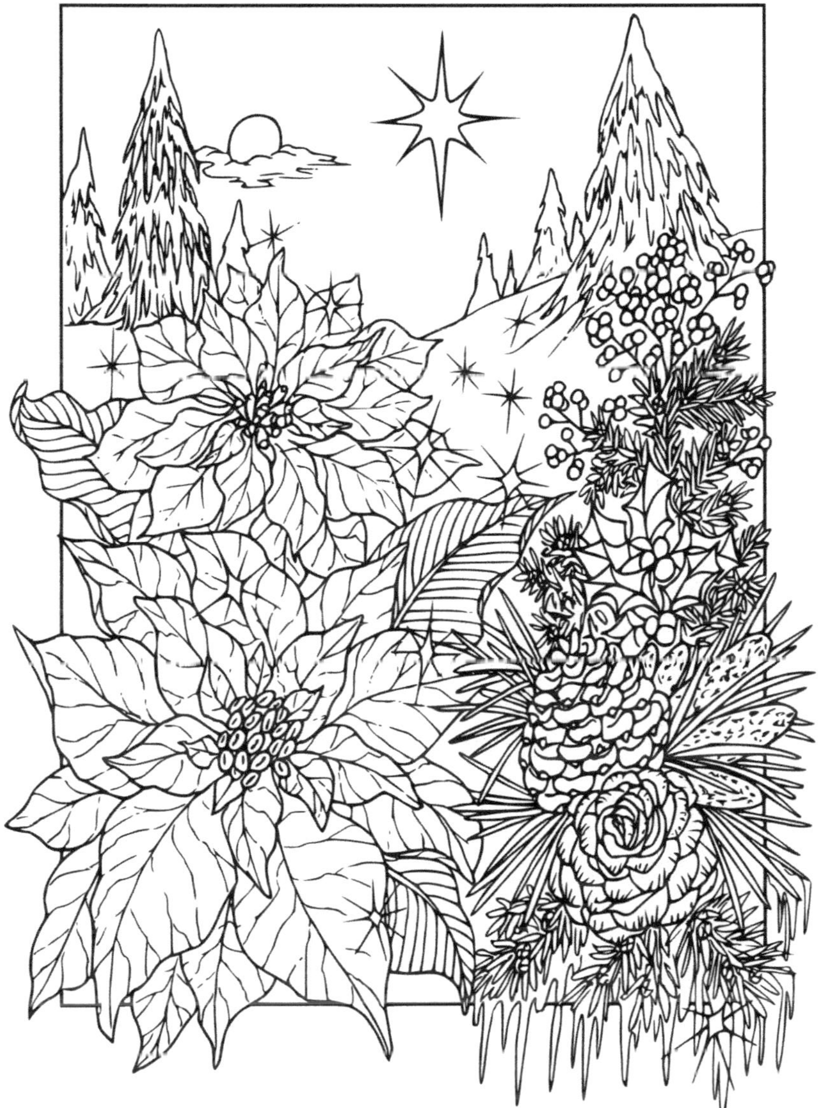

'Spirit of Winter'

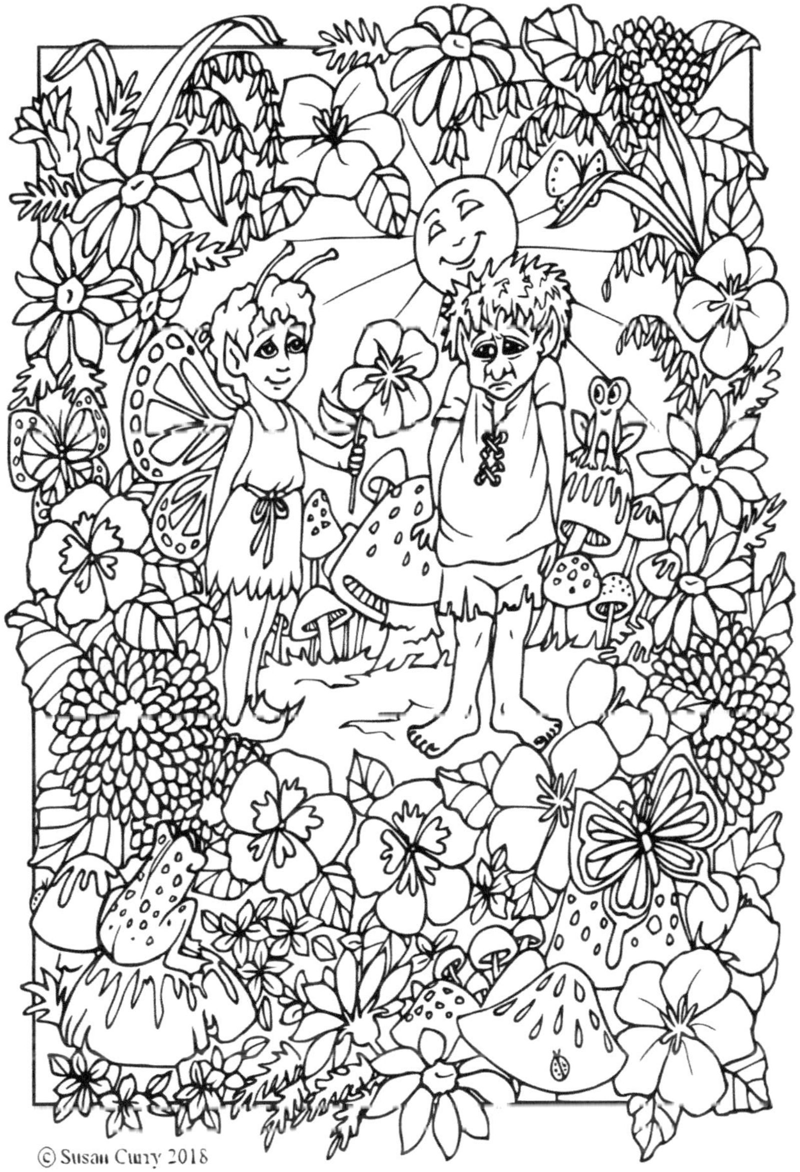

'Let's Be Friends'

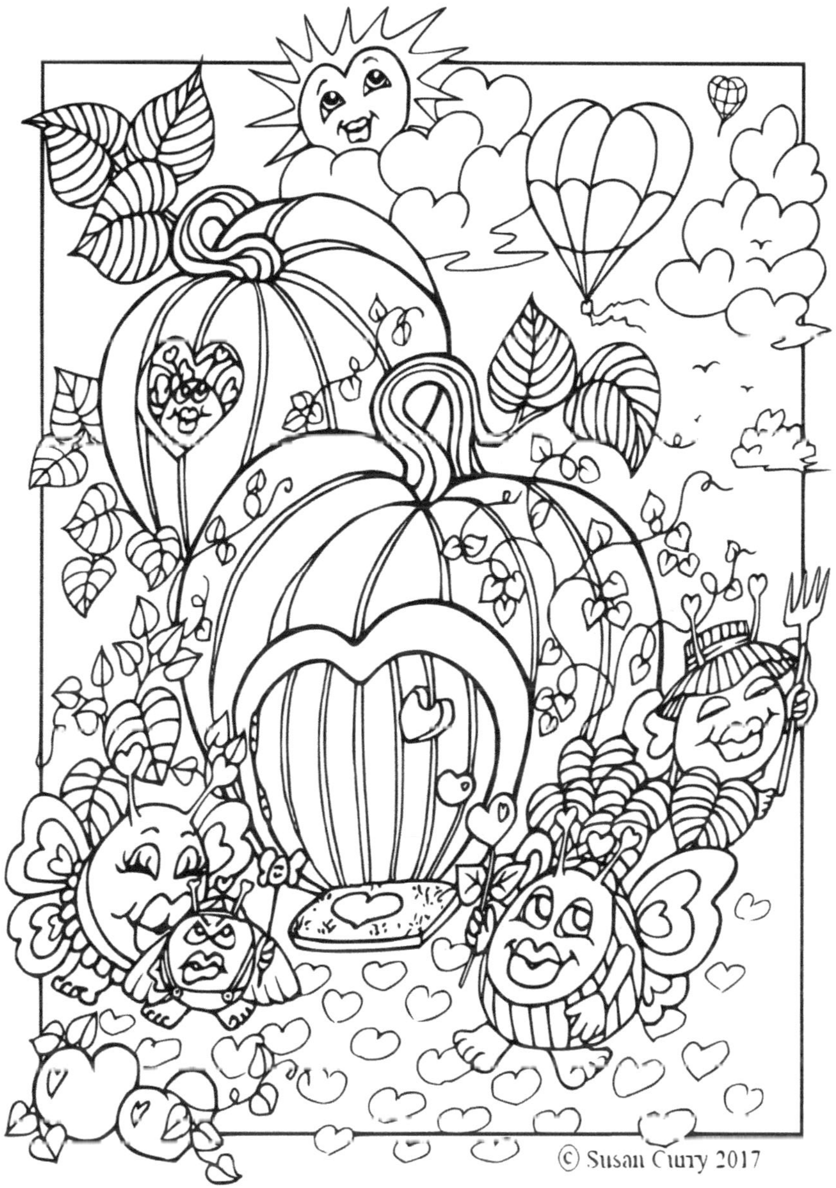

'Mandala Madness' © Susan Cury 2018

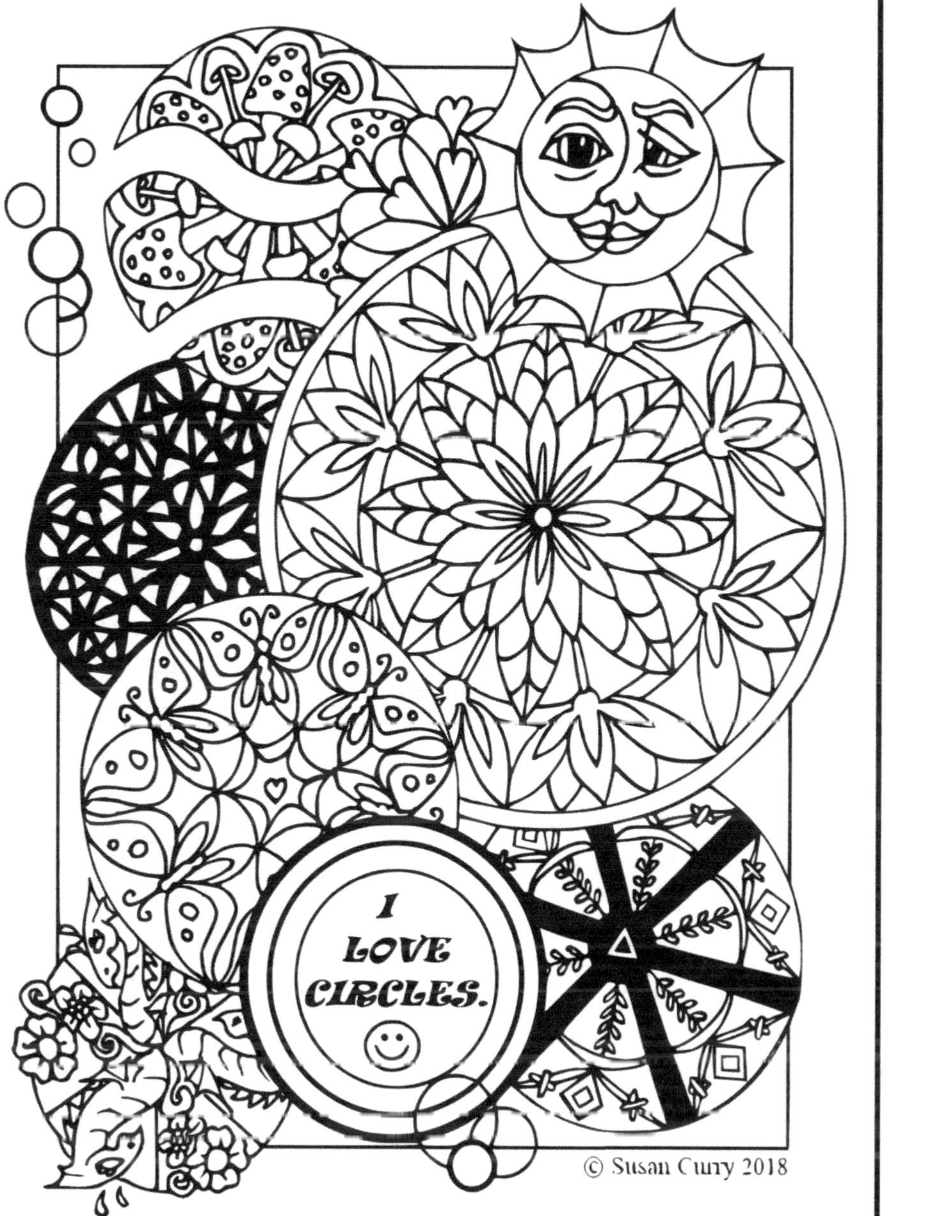

'The Love Bugs' © Susan Cury 2017

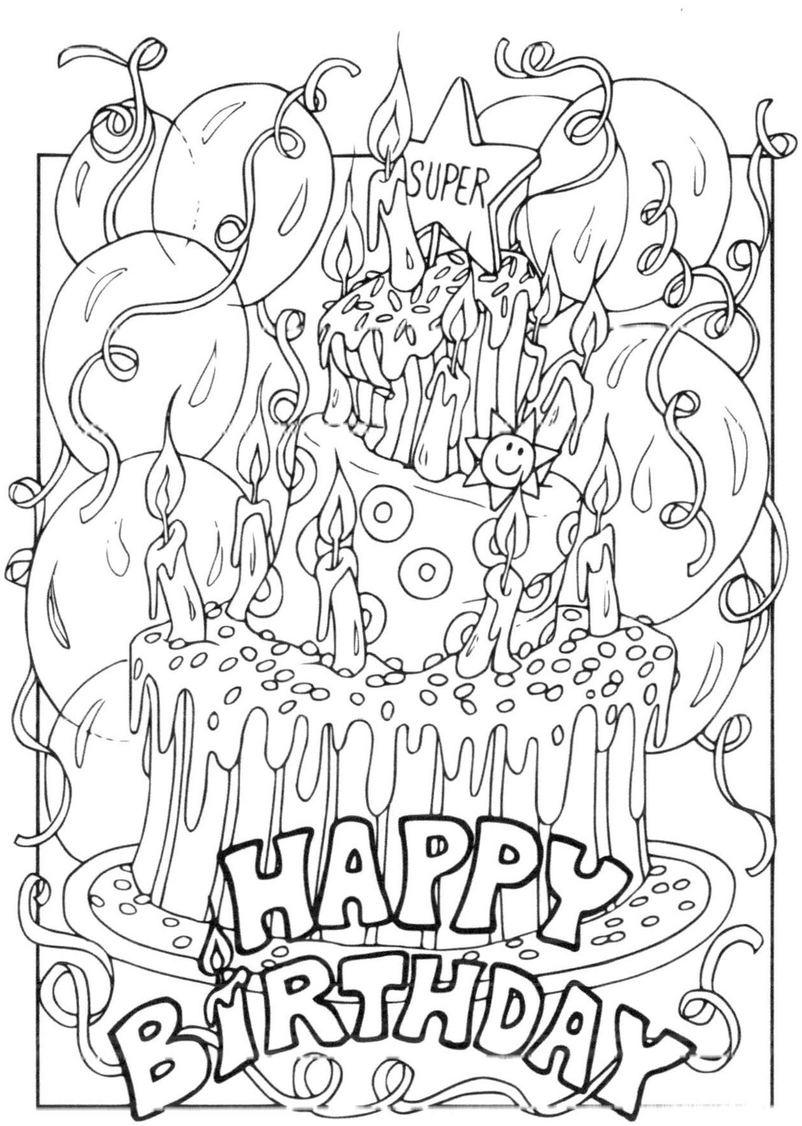

'Happy Easter'

'Happy Birthday'

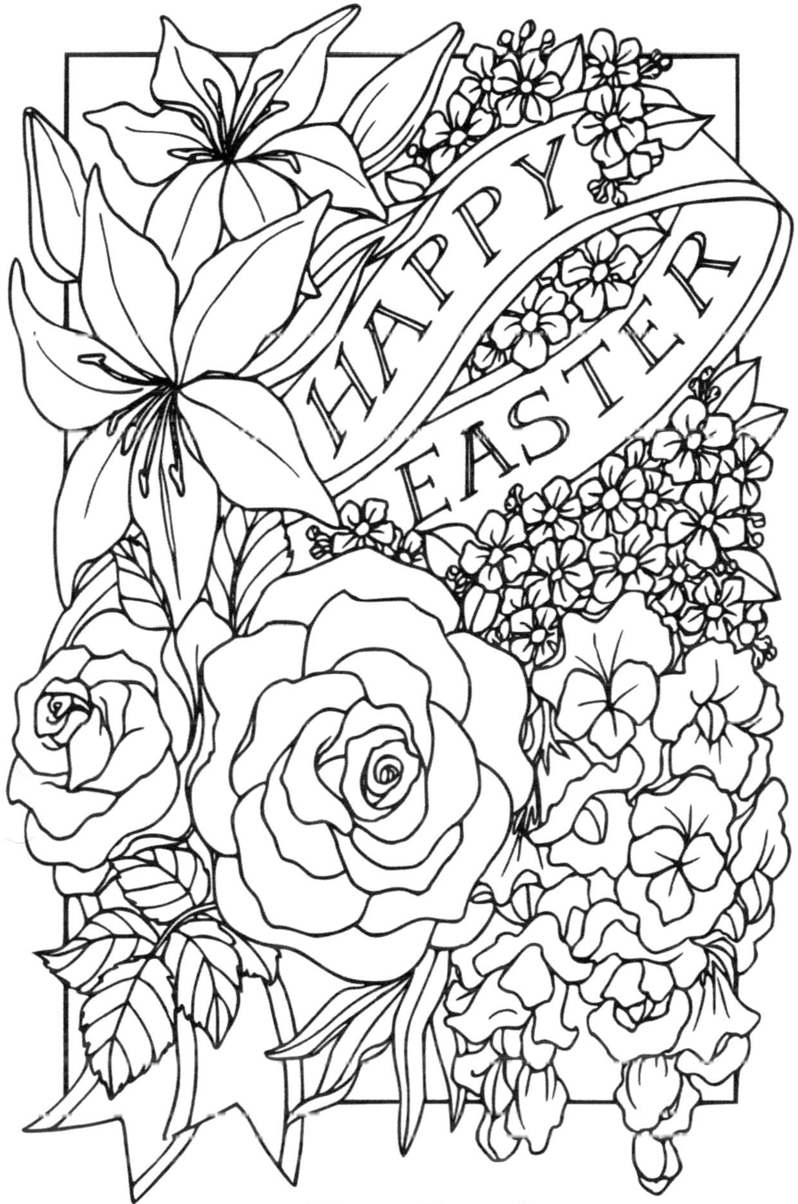

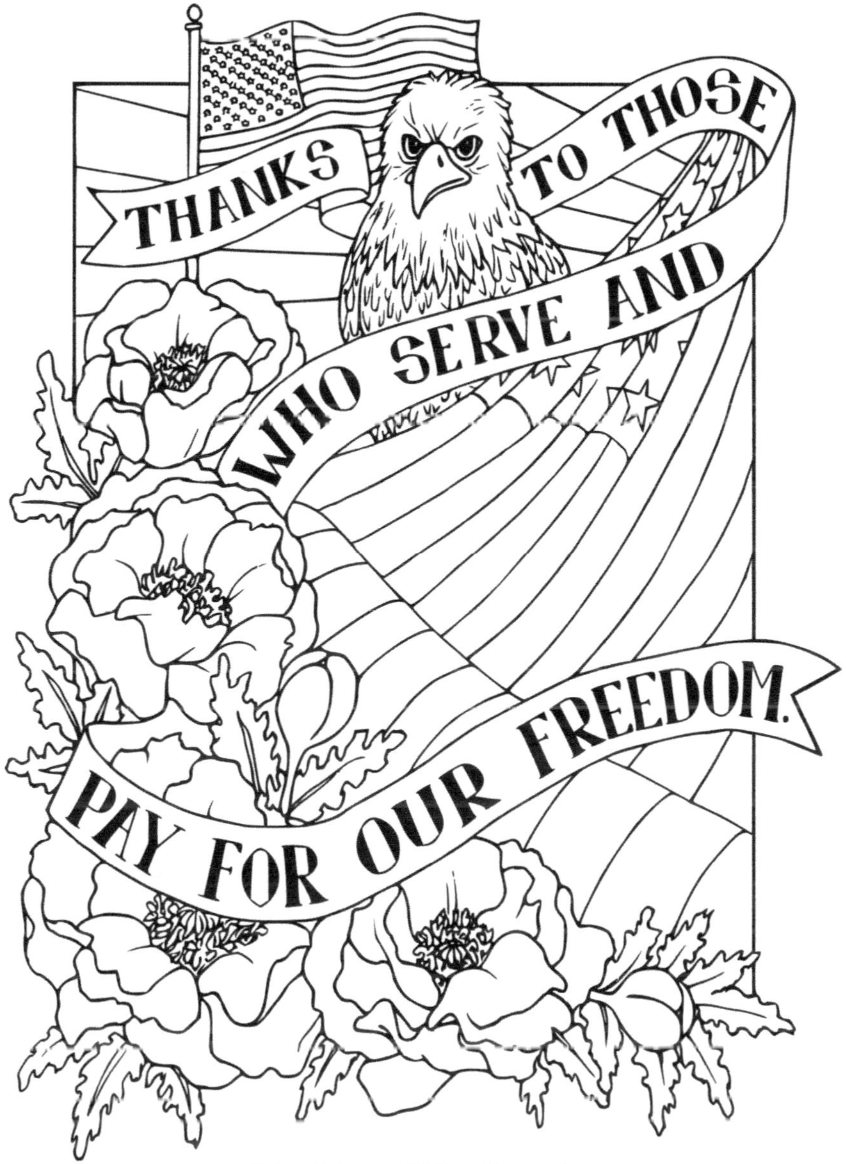

© Susan Curry 2018

Praise Him, from whom all blessings flow.

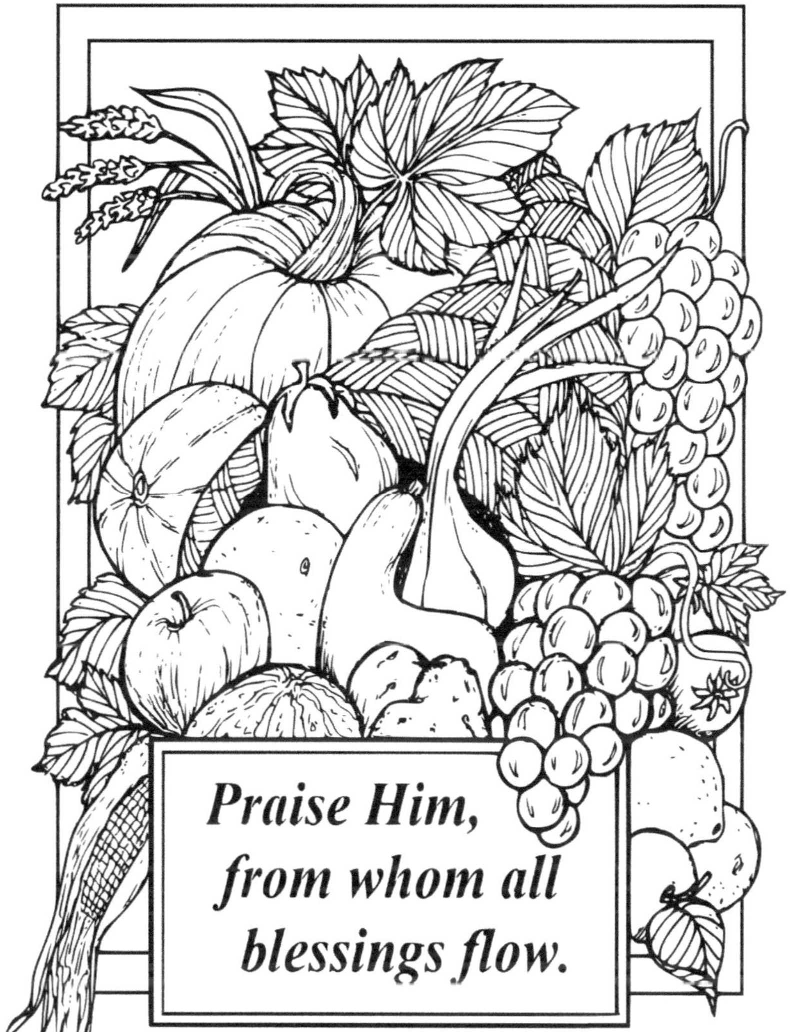

'Thanksgiving'

© Susan Curry 2018

THANKS TO THOSE WHO SERVE AND PAY FOR OUR FREEDOM.

'For Those Who Serve'

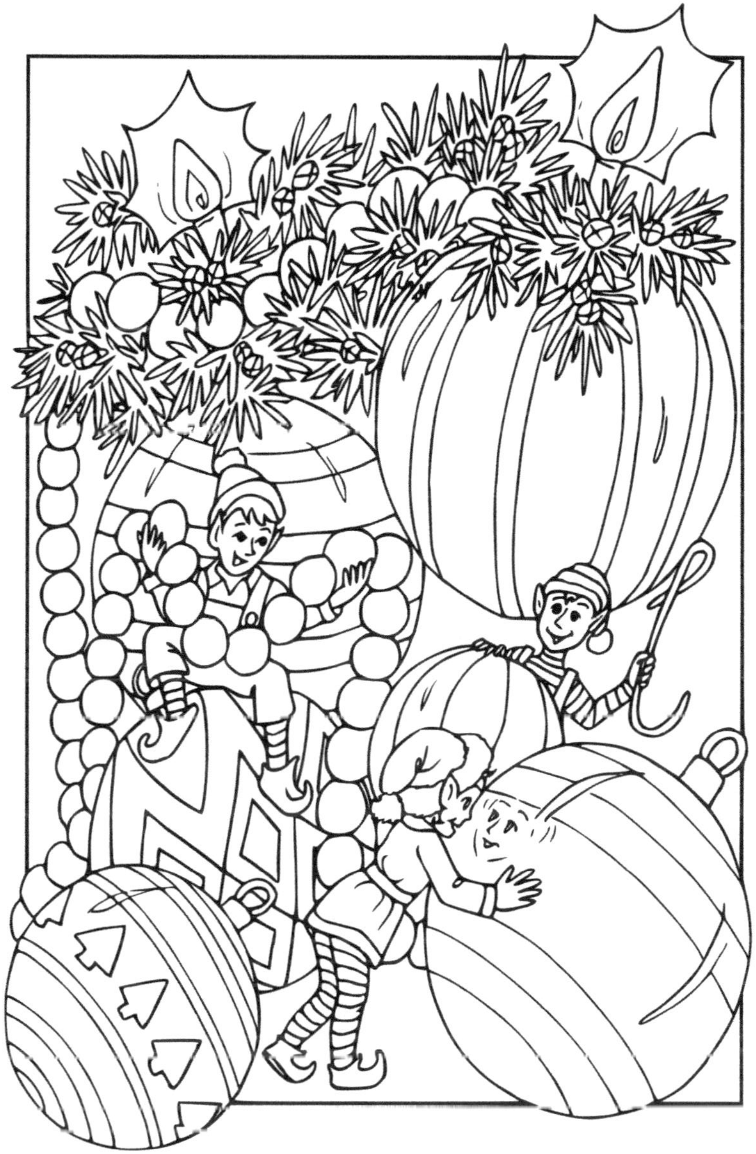

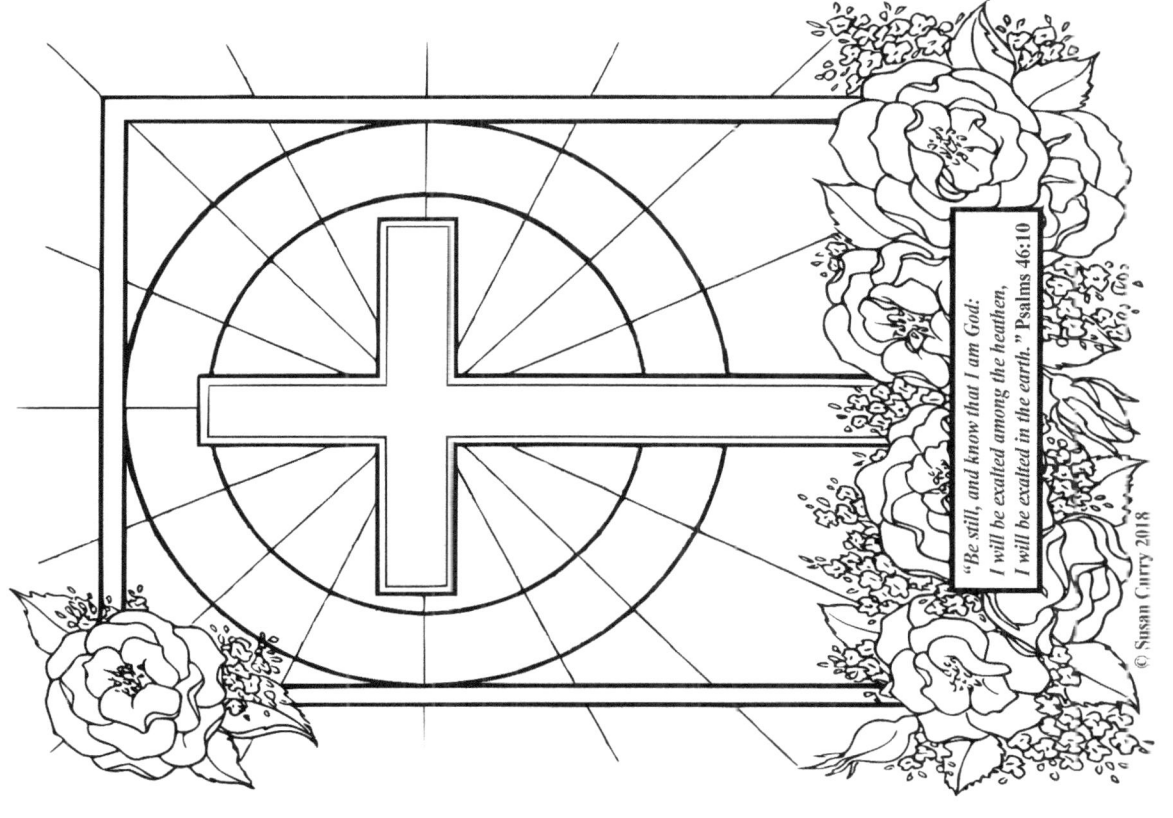

'Be Still and Know'

'Christmas Helpers'

5 BONUS PAGES
from the previous and future works of
Artist Susan Curry

1. *The Scarecrow*
   from "Living on Memory Lane"
2. *The Ballerina*
   from "The Adventures of Little Sister"
3. *Summer Days*
   from "Adventures with Country Cousins"
4. *Poinsettia and Berries*
   from "Christmas on Memory Lane"
5. *Sweet Hour of Prayer*
   a preview page of "Sing, Color and Praise the Lord,"
   coming soon.

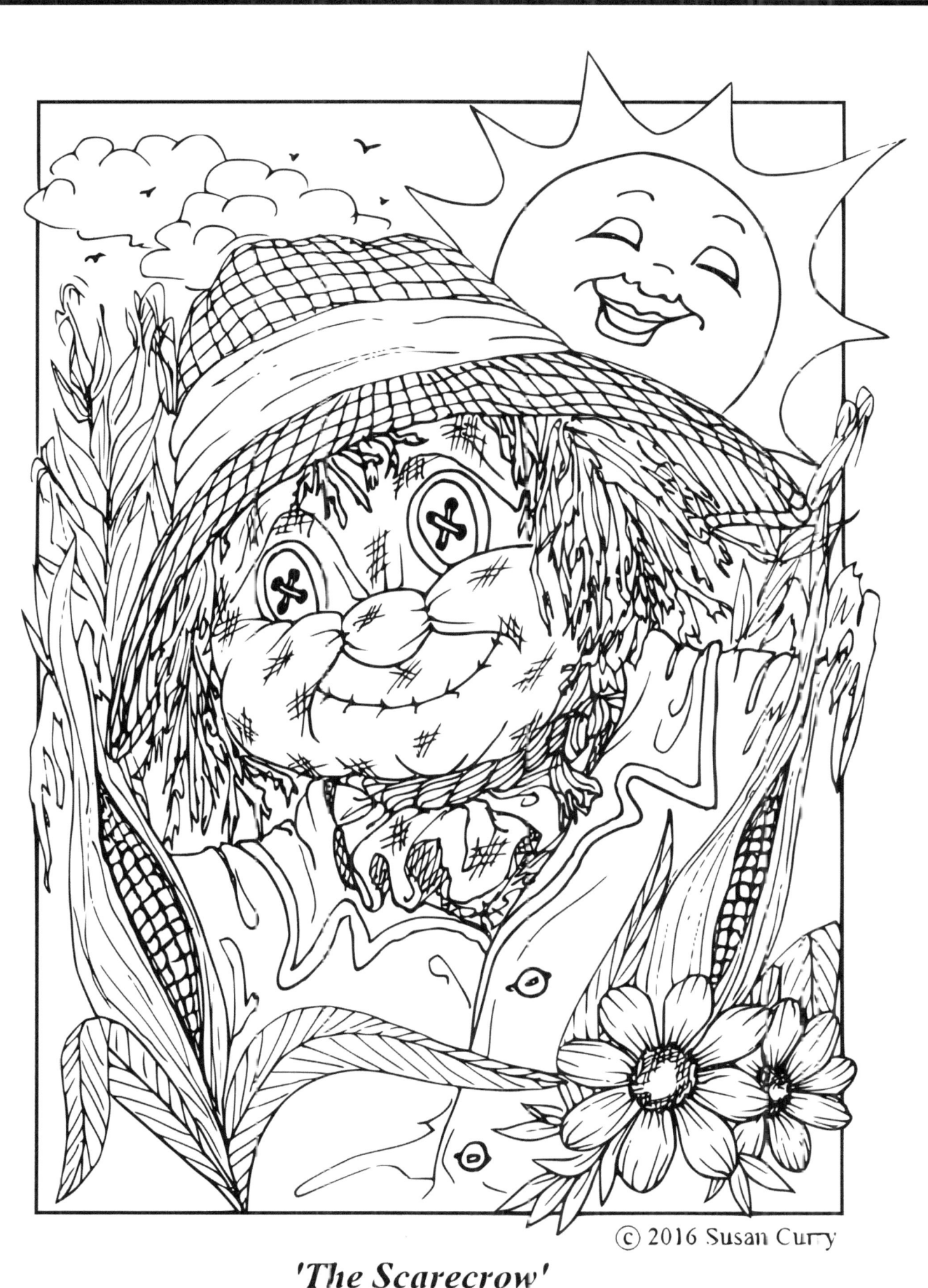

'The Scarecrow'

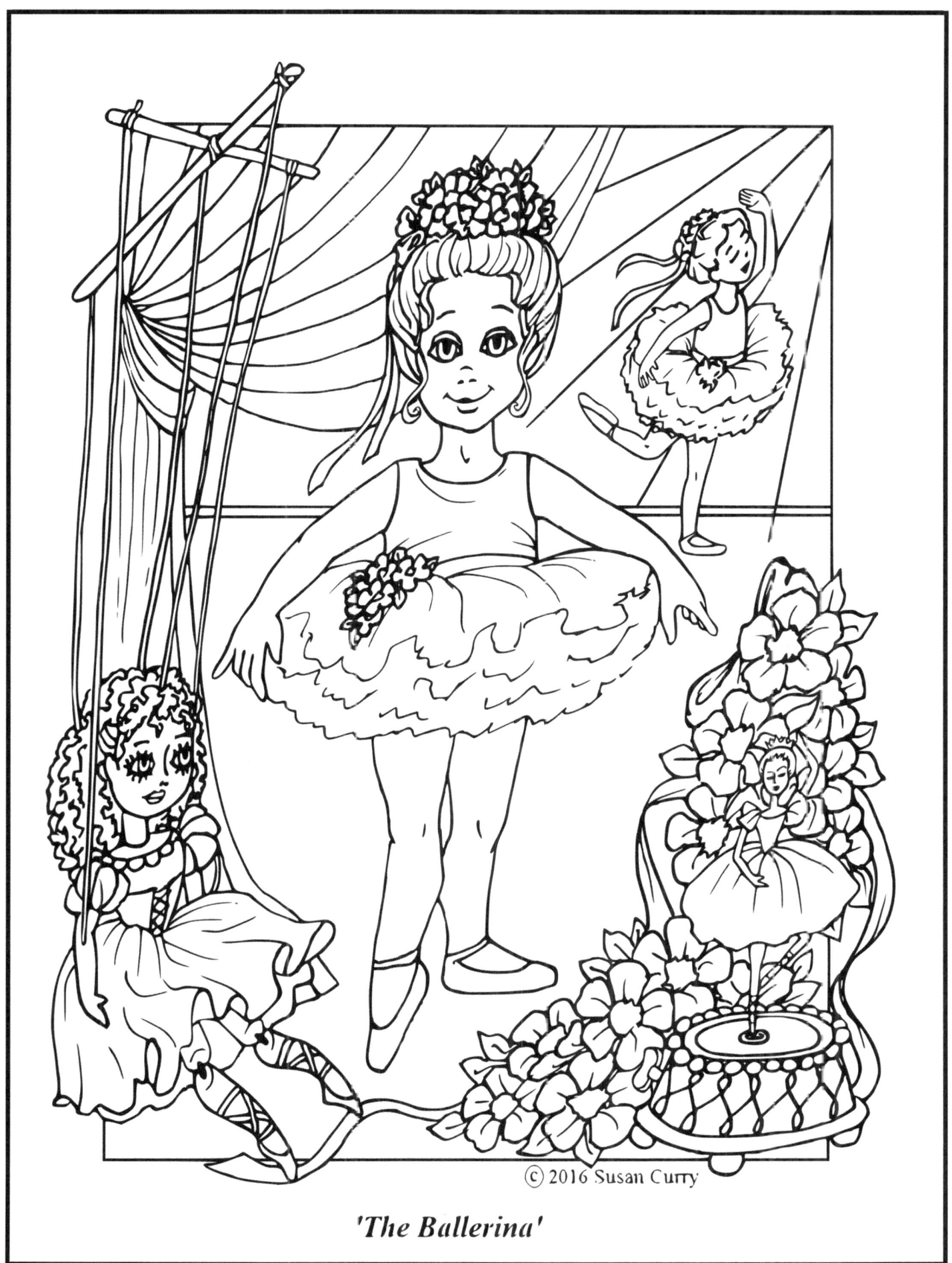

'The Ballerina'

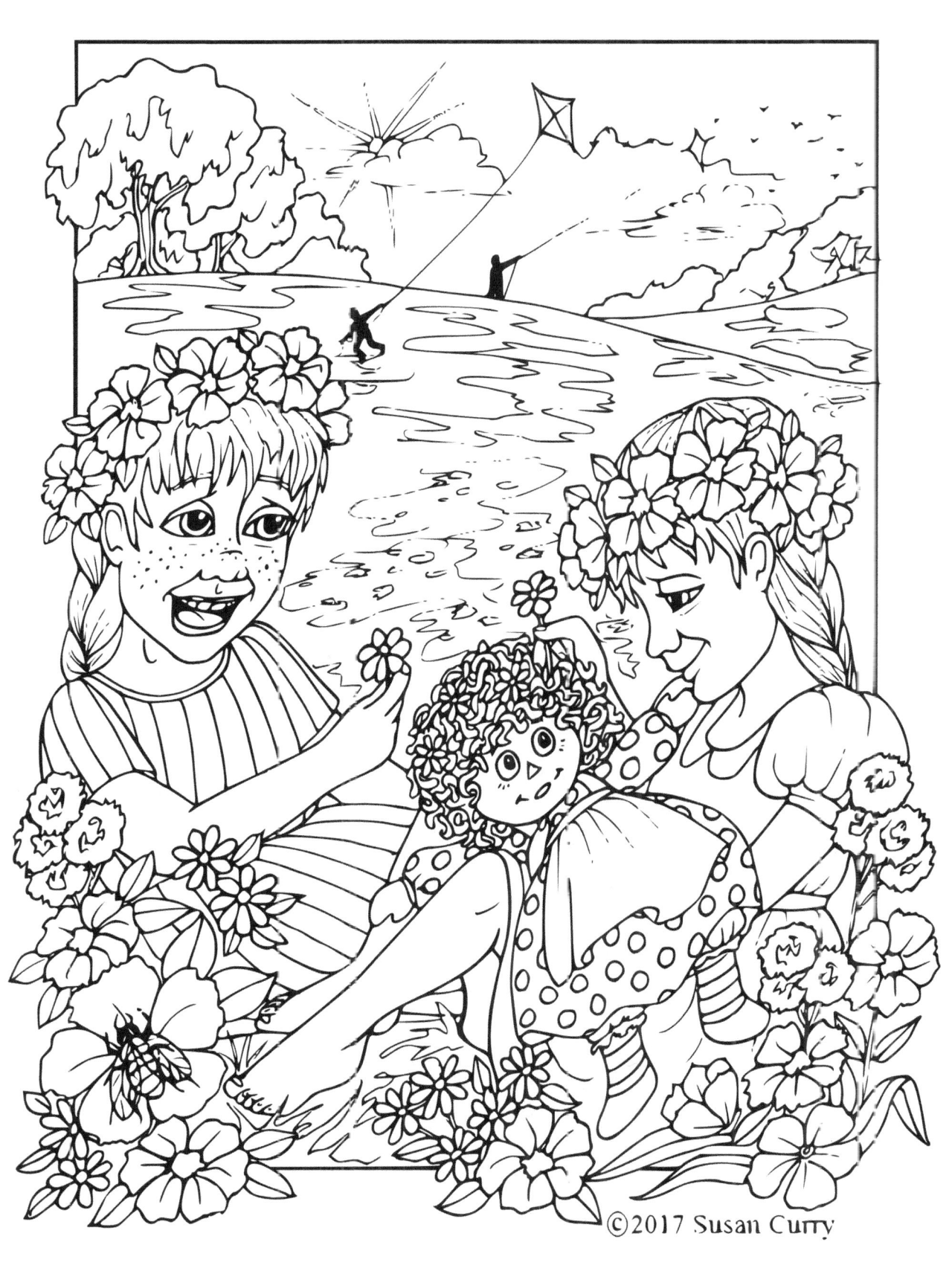

'Summer Days'

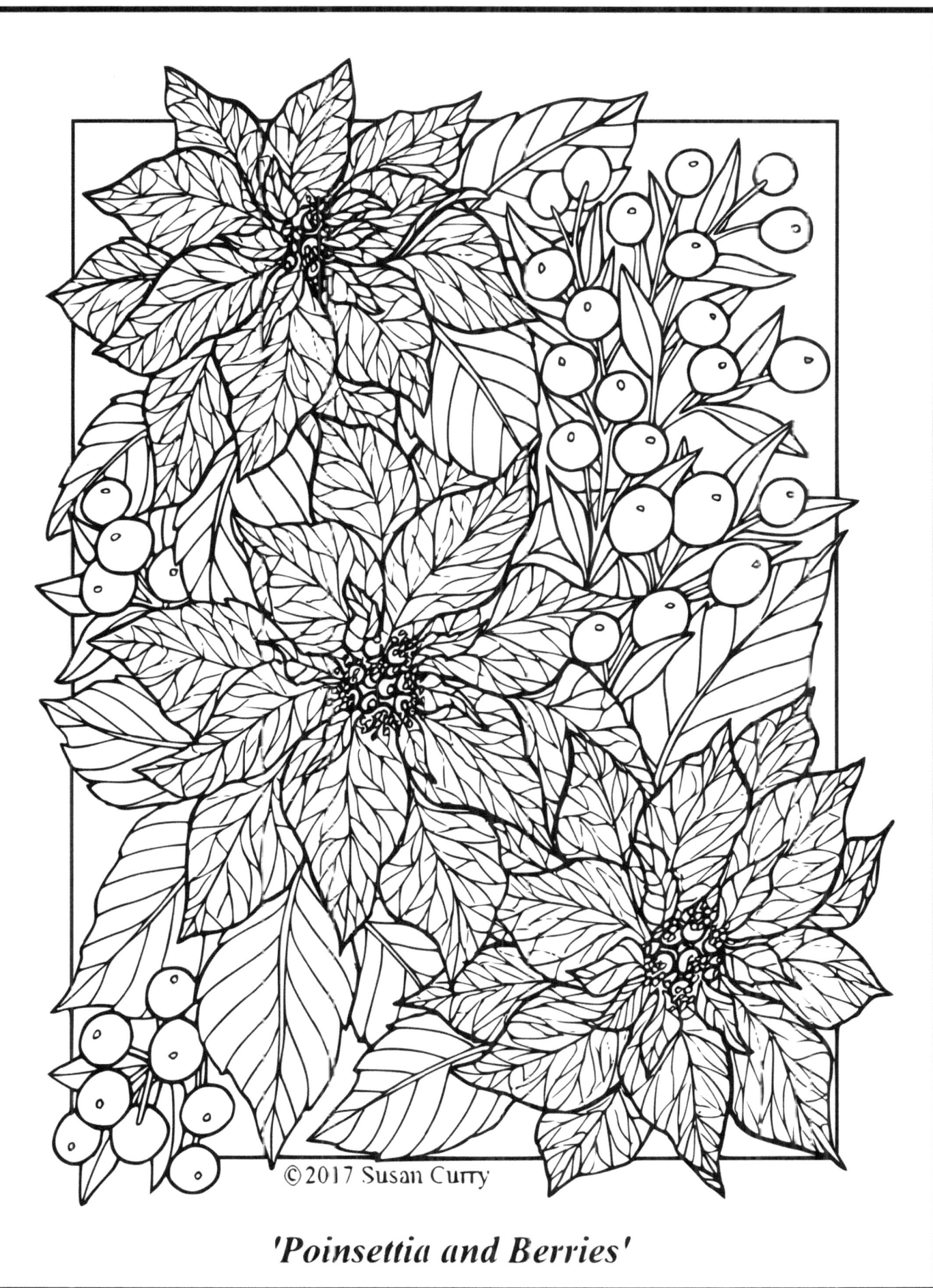

'Poinsettia and Berries'

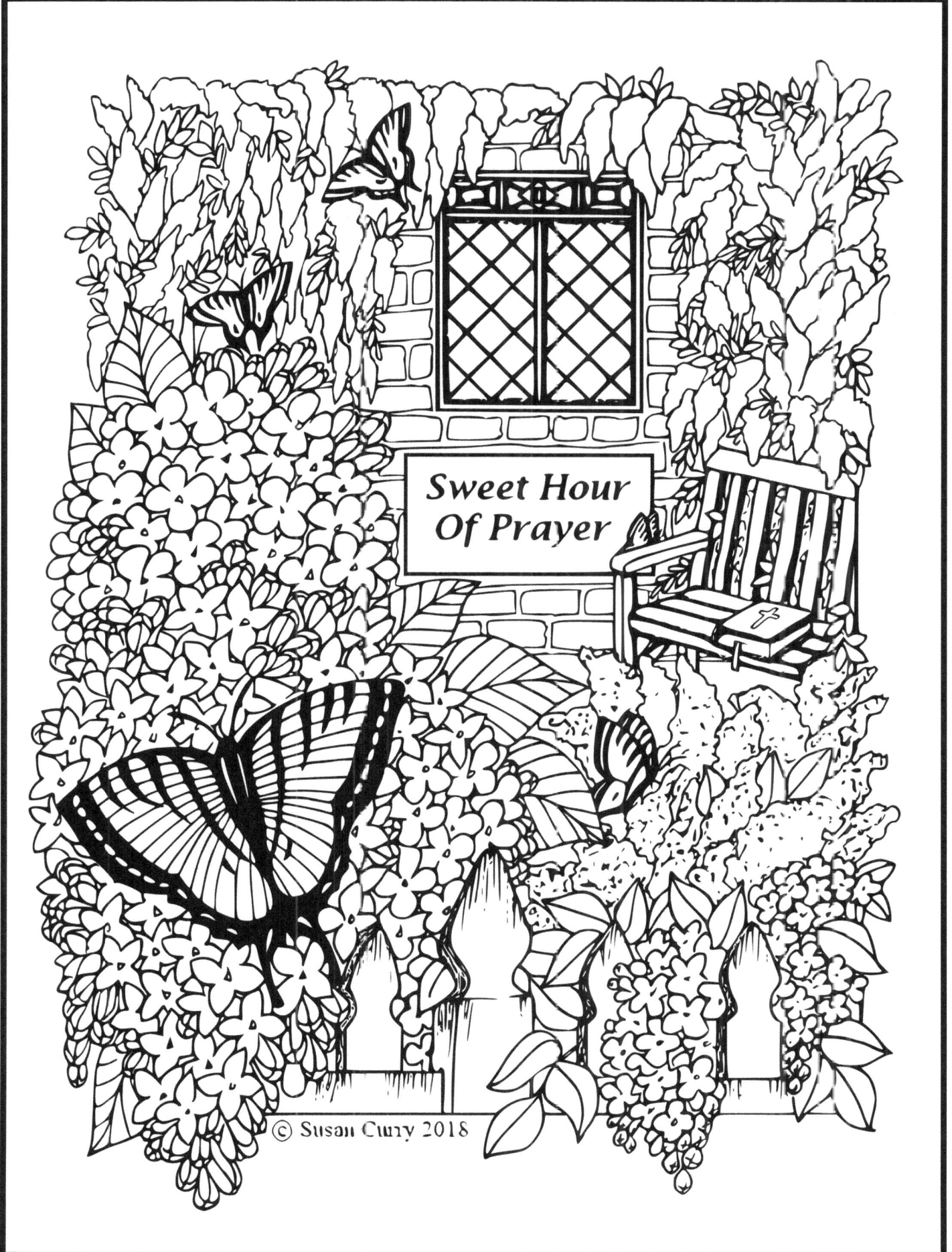

This page has intentionally been left blank for use as either a blotting page or color testing page.

This page has intentionally been left blank for use as either a blotting page or color testing page.

Don't miss my other books

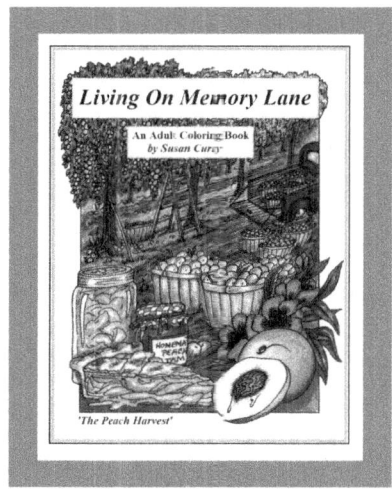
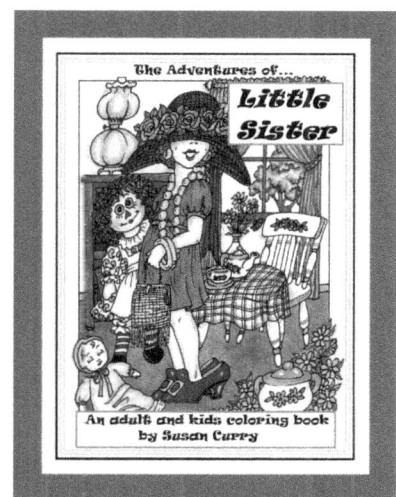
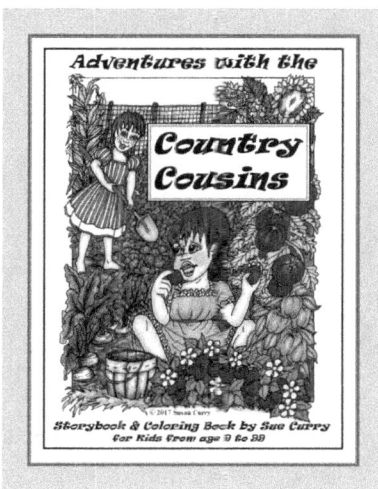
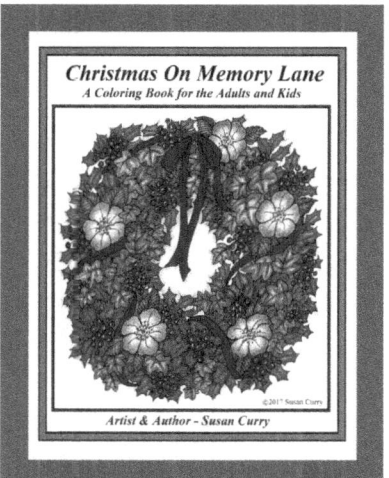

AVAILABLE in print at AMAZON
(worldwide)

or as a printable PDF download
at MemoryLaneArt on Etsy.com

www.ingramcontent.com/pod-product-compliance
Lightning Source LLC
Chambersburg PA
CBHW062332220526
45469CB00008B/2685